Love in Four Dimensions

D1115690

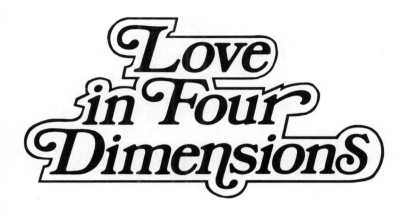

Love in Four Dimensions

William E. Hull

BROADMAN PRESS
Nashville, Tennessee

This is for
John and Virginia Berry

Who taught me more about love
than many books

and for their congregation

The First Baptist Church
New Castle, Kentucky

Who did not despise my youth
when I served them as Pastor
1953—1958

© Copyright 1982 • Broadman Press
All rights reserved.
4253-35
ISBN: 0-8054-5335-0

Dewey Decimal Classification: 231.6
Subject heading: LOVE (THEOLOGY)
Library of Congress Catalog Card Number: 81-68043
Printed in the United States of America

Preface

On July 24, 1955 I preached a sermon entitled
"Love in Four Dimensions" in the First Baptist
Church, New Castle, Kentucky. At the time, I was
not only pastor of that challenging congregation but
also a graduate student studying for doctoral exam-
inations in New Testament. I was also a newly appointed seminary instructor preparing to teach
courses in elementary and intermediate Greek. The
summer was hot; my duties were heavy; the Vaca-
tion Bible School schedule during the previous week
had been hectic; and our first child was almost due.
Thus, that Sunday evening sermon reflected little
more than my hasty embellishment of a clever outline on John 3:16 suggested by a communion meditation of Albert Joseph McCartney. This outline had
been handed to me recently by a helpful parishioner.

Despite such an inauspicious beginning, the sermon was so well received that I began to work on it
in earnest after my pastorate ended and my work
came to involve me almost weekly in supply preaching as a professor and administrator at The Southern
Baptist Theological Seminary, Louisville, Kentucky. Records indicate that over a twenty-five year
period I preached some variation on this sermon

nearly 150 times, in almost every instance revising, enriching, and polishing what had been said before.

As might be expected, in such a process the sermon began to grow to the point that I divided it into two messages, one on God's love to us and another on our response in loving others. Even that structure, however, was inadequate to contain the insights that accumulated through years of reading and speaking on this subject. Therefore, when I came to my present pastorate, the First Baptist Church, Shreveport, Louisiana, I resolved to give my favorite "sugar-stick" the really serious attention which it deserved. The result was a series of six sermons preached between March 14 and April 25, 1976, which corresponds somewhat to the six chapters of this book.

Why have I decided to issue this pulpit material in printed form? Primarily because it has been requested more frequently and more eagerly than anything else I have ever done. For reasons not entirely clear to me, my sermons on John 3:16 seem to have blessed more people than any other messages which I have preached. That is not a polite form of self-congratulation but an honest appraisal of what God has been pleased to honor insofar as I can determine it from the response of hundreds of congregations in which I have sought to minister.

It has given me special pleasure to discharge this stewardship of setting forth my best word on God's love in more permanent form. Much of my writing has been historical and technical. Thus I have relished the change of pace in preparing something more theological and devotional. I have usually written for scholars and well-trained pastors, but it will be a joy if these meditations are found useful by a wider circle of ministers and laypersons. Some may think it strange to mix popular homiletical material with careful points of Greek grammar, but I find it especially exciting to carry the interpretative process all of the way from the most rigorous study of primary texts to a medium which is meaningful to those with no interest in biblical scholarship.

I have once again to thank my congregation both for the high privilege of hammering out this material in the pulpit and for the generous study-leave program which provided an uninterrupted opportunity to put my thoughts on paper. As before, the James P. Boyce Centennial Library of The Southern Baptist Theological Seminary, through Librarian Ronald F. Deering, has shown me every courtesy in providing the resources needed to underpin the foundations of this work. Ann Eastepp, Sheila MacKnight, and Aljean Middleton have continued their high level of craftsmanship in preparing a manuscript for the publisher.

At least once in mid-career, every preacher should pause to set forth the heart of his gospel. Insofar as I am able, this effort accomplishes that purpose. I will rejoice if my witness sheds light on the central mystery of the Christian faith for those willing to receive it. This book goes forth in the hope that it will enable you to have the same kind of experience as Joyce Cary's curate in *The Captive and the Free:*

> "I was suddenly moved to understand the thing that had stood before my eyes all my

life, as wide as the world, as high as the sky, the thing I had repeated a thousand times in prayers and in sermons without understanding, the miracle of God's love in the world."[1]

WILLIAM E. HULL
Shreveport, Louisiana

Note

1. Quoted by Douglas Stewart, "Three Conversions," *The Expository Times* 72 (January, 1961):122.

Contents

   I. "What Wondrous Love Is This?".....13

  II. The Breadth of God's Love.........29

 III. The Length of God's Love..........49

 IV. The Depth of God's Love...........65

  V. The Height of God's Love..........83

 VI. The Ultimate Dimension...........97

The Texts

For this cause I kneel before the Father from whom every family in heaven and on earth takes its name, that he would grant to all of you in full measure, out of the riches of his glory, a mighty strengthening through the reinforcement of the Spirit in the inner life. I further pray that Christ may make his home in your hearts through faith in such a way that his love will take root and become your firm foundation, to the end that you will be empowered to grasp together with all of God's People the dimensions of that love: *"the Breadth" and "the Length" and "the Depth" and "the Height"*—that you may indeed know the love of Christ, even though it surpasses knowledge, and knowing it that you will be filled with all the fullness of God! (Eph. 3:14-19).

Here is how much God lavished his love on the world: he actually gave up his uniquely beloved Son in order that each and every person placing personal trust in him need not perish but possess the life of the New Age that endures forever (John 3:16).

Translations by William E. Hull

I
"What Wondrous Love Is This?"

In 1877 archaeologists unearthed from the sands of Egypt a pink granite shaft which was popularly dubbed "Cleopatra's Needle."[1] When the maze of hieroglyphics covering the column had been deciphered, it told the story of a civilization long forgotten — as if a giant that had slept for nearly thirty-five centuries was suddenly awakened to tell tales of a distant past. Plans were made to erect the obelisk during the following year on the Thames embankment in the heart of London as a gift to the British people. Before preparations could be completed, however, the realization dawned that one day England might be a memory. The Comte de Volney, in his *Les Ruines,* had pictured a future historian wandering along the Thames looking amid the rubble for significant clues of what had been St. Paul's Cathedral and Nelson's Monument.[2]

In anticipation of a distant era when London might be as Heliopolis, and the shaft once again resurrected to stand in some new metropolis, a committee was appointed to place at the base of the obelisk a time deposit box.[3] Into this vault went representative reflections of contemporary life: a set of coinage; specimens of weights and measures;

children's toys; a London city directory; a bundle of
newspapers; photographs of the twelve most beautiful women of the period; various articles of feminine
adornment; and a translation of the hieroglyphics.
But what provision could be made for the faith of
the people? Obviously, they could not cram into that
capsule a vaulting cathedral, or — much as they
might have liked it — seal up a stuffy bishop! How do
you best put religion in a box as a legacy for generations yet unborn? The committee decided to select
the most important verse in the Bible, and to include
it in the 215 known languages of that day.[4]

1

Suppose it had been your assignment to choose
the greatest single sentence in Scripture. Is there
among the mountain peaks of inspired utterance a
Mount Everest that towers above them all? Although we could bear testimony to many passages
that have been a lamp to our feet and a light to our
path (Ps. 119:105), I believe that we would finally
come to the same consensus as did the committee
stocking the repository in Cleopatra's Needle.

For Christians in every age have venerated one
verse as the most comprehensive expression of the
central thrust of the biblical message.[5] Far from
being the proof text for any one doctrine or denomi-
nation, it is the climactic text which holds all of our
beliefs and practices together. As the verse which
we learn first and forget last, this one sentence can
lay fair claim to being the most familiar and beloved
utterance in all of Christendom.

Its unique familiarity is fraught, however, not only with promise but with peril. The words have become slick from frequent usage as they run down the well-cut grooves of memory. Although we know them by heart, they have a way of rolling off the mind without jabbing the conscience or stinging the emotions. It was said of Bernard Berenson that he possessed to the highest degree "the power of seeing everything each day as if it had never been seen before."[6] Somehow we need to get behind the years of commonplace companionship with our text and hear its words as if we had never heard them before. By an exercise of spiritual and historical imagination, try to reproduce in the here-and-now that thrill of discovery which must have overwhelmed those in the long ago to whom the incredible claim first came: "For God so loved the world that he gave his only Son, that whoever believes in him should not perish but have eternal life" (John 3:16, RSV).

Surely this is the most exquisite flower in the garden of Holy Scripture. "Deep calls to deep" (Ps. 42:7, RSV); "grace is heaped up upon grace" (John 1:16, AT). In its every phrase are vistas that have no end at all but run out beyond the rim of the mind and melt into the far reaches of eternity.[7] "Centuries may come and go, empires may rise and fall, but these words will speak forevermore with fadeless charm to the hungry hearts of men."[8] In any possible age, this one seed would be sufficient to secure the Gospel in the affections of the human race. Never have words been penned that are more incandescent in clarity, breathtaking in beauty, inexhaustible in power, and enduring in strength. Here is truth so profound and infinite, yet so tender and personal, that the lips quiver to utter it.

What, then, shall the preacher say? In the presence of such grandeur, does not any comment seem superfluous, an audacity and impertinence? Is there a single syllable in this sentence that our embarrassed stammerings could explain or enhance? Meanings continually erupt from these subterranean depths and overflow the little cups that we bring to contain them. In the presence of such immensities we are moved to exclaim with the apostle Paul, "O the depth of the riches and wisdom and knowledge of God!" (Rom. 11:33, RSV).

When Jane Burden first sat for William Morris, the artist toiled for a time with his paints to no avail. At last he was forced to show her, not a finished picture, but a canvas with these words, "I cannot paint you but I love you."[9] Just so, the interpreter who stares at these words long enough will finally find himself "Lost in wonder, love, and praise."[10]

For years I sat speechless before our text, much as my infant son sat captivated by the ceaseless breakers washing up upon the shore the first time he saw the sea. Nor was I alone in this tribute of silence. A ministerial colleague, disconcerted by the realization that he had never once preached on John 3:16, searched the eleven volumes of the *American Pulpit Series* and discovered that seventy of his contemporaries had not done so either, nor had the pulpit giants of the past whom he consulted.[11] His conclusion is one which I share, that even the best of preachers can be overawed by a verse whose simplicity seems to warrant no comment and whose sublimity seems to defy it!

And, yet, this verse both intimidates and invites as it reposes on the pedestal where the ages have placed it. When the British explorer, George Leigh Mallory, who finally died in a 1924 assault on Mount Everest, was asked why he would risk life and limb to scale the 29,028 foot peak, he replied simply, "Because it is there."[12] Just so, because John 3:16 is *there*, something within us fairly cries out to explore its terrain. If only we could reach that lofty summit, the reward would be an unparalleled vantage point from which to view the entire sweep of biblical revelation. Is there a way to scale those heights without either belaboring the obvious or trivializing the profound?

2

While pondering that problem, I came upon a majestic prayer of the apostle Paul which struggles with the very same challenge (Eph. 3:14-19). Once Christ comes to make his home in the human heart through faith (v. 17*a*), the soil in which life is now rooted, the foundation on which it now rests, is that of love (v. 17*b*). But this undergirding reality must not go unnoticed, or be taken for granted, or be treated as a vague emotional impulse. How glibly we use the word *love* to cover a multitude of moods! And so Paul went on to pray that his readers might be empowered to "comprehend"—literally, to "get down" clearly in their understanding—what this love supplied by the presence of Christ really means (v. 18*a*). In other words, there is to be not only a *grounding* in love to the *bottom* of our *hearts* but also a *grasping* of love to the *top* of our *minds!*

At this point the apostle added an important quali-
fication: "with all the saints" (RSV), by which he re-
ferred, not to a special group of "super-Christians,"
as we sometimes use the term, but rather, as *The
New English Bible* puts it, to "all God's people," the
church (v. 18*b*). Two important truths are balanced
here. On the one hand, deepest reality is not reserved for a few specialists. God's love is not so com-
plicated that it requires rabbis or theologians to an-
alyze its nature, nor so esoteric that it needs Gnos-
tics or apocalyptists to unravel its secrets. On the
other hand, it is so profound that the entire house-
hold of faith must think and pray and share together
very deeply in order to fathom its meaning. Put
simply: *Any* Christian may climb this spiritual Mount
Everest, but he or she dare not attempt it *alone!*

What sort of guidelines are provided for a company of believers in quest of insight regarding the
central reality of their experience with Christ? Almost abruptly Paul asserted that to truly apprehend
God's love we must explore its "breadth, and length,
and depth, and height" (v. 18*c*, KJV). Long ago the
author of the Book of Job had exclaimed (11:7-9,
RSV):

Can you find out the deep things of God?
Can you find out the limit of the Almighty?
It is *higher* than heaven—what can you do?
Deeper than Sheol—what can you know?
Its measure is *longer* than the earth,
     and *broader* than the sea (author's italics).

Taking his cue from the biblical heritage, rather
than from Greek thought which distinguished only

three dimensions,[13] Paul bade his readers grasp the inexhaustible sweep of God's love. It was as if he invited them to look in every direction: to the vaulting skies above; to the plunging depths of the sea below; to every horizon whether north, east, south, or west; and suddenly to realize — *the love of Christ is as large as that!* Paul's stress on the all-encompassing dimensions of Christ's love was not geometrical or astrological but theological and poetical. "He is simply trying to express with rhetorical fullness the magnitude of the vision which opens before Christian faith as it seeks to comprehend the ways of God: there is no region of the universe that is not embraced in his purpose and governed by his love."[14]

The results of comprehending divine love are as staggering as that love itself. Ephesians 3:19 describes two such fruits in climactic fashion. First, we will "know the love of Christ which surpasses knowledge" (v. 19*a*, RSV). In the Old Testament, there are no final answers to the questions of Job. The infinity of God only underscores his inscrutability. But Paul, while affirming the limitlessness of divine love that defies human containment, nevertheless injected into his prayer a logical contradiction by insisting that we can actually *know* the love of Christ even though, because of its vastness, such love is utterly *unknowable*. The only resolution of that paradox comes by realizing that such understanding is nothing less than a miracle, that is, a gift of divine revelation. It is completely beyond our human ability to grasp the love of Christ, but God's Spirit in our hearts (v. 16) supplies the "power to comprehend" (v. 18*a*, RSV) that which would otherwise be incomprehensible.

As if that were not enough, our text goes on to indicate that we are to attain the unattainable knowledge of Christ's love so as to "be filled with all the fulness of God" (v. 19b, RSV). Love has just been said to have four dimensions, in an effort to pay tribute to its "fulness." Now we see that to "comprehend" divine fullness (v. 18a, RSV) leads to the possibility of experiencing that fullness within our human lives. God's love is not an abstract idea to be analyzed by the mind. It is a living presence filling the totality of life. With God's love in our hearts, we begin to live in a more spacious environment. Our thoughts take on a greater breadth of perspective; our actions go to greater lengths of endurance; our feelings plumb greater depths of meaning; our spirits soar to greater heights of fulfillment. God's love does not constrict our experience but liberates it for limitless growth.[15]

It is an audacious prayer that Paul has recorded in Ephesians 3:14-19, particularly in the way that it climbs the "steep ascent of heav'n" in so few verses. Beginning with human "faith" in v. 17 ("that Christ may dwell in your hearts through *faith,*" RSV, author's italics), it ends with divine "fulness" only two verses later ("that you may be filled with all the *fulness* of God," v. 19, RSV). Think of it! From our emptiness to his filling, from our passivity to his activity, from our weakness to his power—and all of that is possible if we have an intimate grasp of the manifold implications of God's love.

We meet this staggering leap from "faith" to "fulness" not only in Ephesians but in the Gospel of John as well. Its Prologue (John 1:1-18) pivots on the contention that "all who have *faith*" in Christ (v. 12, AT) not only behold the incarnate Word as one "full of grace and truth" (v. 14, RSV) but also themselves, "from that *fullness*," receive grace without measure (v. 16, AT). This parallel manner of describing the Christian life as a pilgrimage from "faith" to "fullness" suggests that there may be significant affinities between the Ephesian Epistle and what has often been called the Ephesian Gospel.[16]

3

In Ephesians 3:18, Paul has provided us with the clue to a comprehension of divine love but not with its content. That is, he has sketched in outline form the need to know love in four dimensions: breadth, length, depth, and height. But he has not told us anything about the substance of these dimensions. Thus, we turn from his prayer convinced that we must somehow discern the meaning of each of these four facets but lacking any guidance from Paul as to just how this might be done.

It is precisely at this point that John 3:16 comes back into focus. For in its familiar phrases we find an adequate definition of every dimension of God's love. That is, John 3:16 provides the content for which Ephesians 3:18 provides the clue. Herein lies the greatness of the most famous verse in the Bible: *It tells us all we need to know about the love of God!*

When, following Ephesians 3:18, we ask, "How *broad* is the love of God?" John 3:16 replies, "For God so loved *the world....*" When we ask, "To what *length* did God go to love a world like ours?" John

3:16 replies, "He gave up his *only Son.*" When we
ask, "To what *depth* did that Son descend on our
behalf?" John 3:16 replies, "He went where people
were *perishing.*" And, finally, when we ask, "To
what *height* did he lift those who were perishing in
the depths?" John 3:16 replies, "He provided them
with *eternal life.*"[17]

The meshing of our two texts in this manner need
not imply either that John was consciously providing a summary of Paul's four love-dimensions or that
Paul was meditating on the structure of this particular verse in John. Rather, we may dare to make a
connection that was not original to either writer
simply because the resulting combination enhances
the contribution which both verses together make to
our understanding of the love of God. In one sense,
we may become bold enough to preach on John 3:16
by using an outline provided by the apostle Paul.
Ephesians 3:18 is like a key that unlocks the riches
awaiting those willing to discover the greatness of
John 3:16 instead of dismissing it as a childhood
relic.

In the chapters that follow, we shall take each of
Paul's love-dimensions in turn and ask what light is
shed upon it by the relevant affirmation in John
3:16. As we do so, the desire will not be to construct
a theoretical concept but rather to facilitate the
prayer of Paul for experiential comprehension, to
the end that all God's people will be filled with the
fullness of his love!

Notes

1. Basic information is provided in *Encyclopaedia Britannica*, 1953, 5:801; 16:667. There were two Egyptian obelisks so named, the other being in Central Park, New York City.

2. Cited in relation to the erection of Cleopatra's Needle in London by Albert Joseph McCartney, "Communion Meditation," *National Presbyterian Church Pulpit*, 1st ser., no. 6 (June, 1954), p. 3.

3. The following is based on an eyewitness account (at the age of six!) by F. W. Boreham, "Everybody's Text," *A Handful of Stars* (New York: Abingdon, 1922), pp. 250-252. Apparently, this is the source on which McCartney was dependent, pp. 3-4.

4. The figure of 215 languages is from Boreham, p. 252. For some reason, McCartney uses the figure of 220 languages. In the Westinghouse Time Capsules buried at the close of the two New York's World Fairs and addressed to the year AD 6939 there are complete copies of the Bible, the King James Version having been deposited after the 1939 fair and the Revised Standard Version after the 1964-65 fair.

5. A fortnight before his death, Martin Luther exclaimed of John 3:16, "What Spartan saying can be compared with this wonderful brevity? It is a Bible in itself!" Cited in Boreham, p. 259.

6. Iris Origo, "The Insatiable Traveler: Bernard Berenson's Quest," *The Atlantic Monthly*, April, 1960, p. 59.

7. Adapted from Arthur John Gossip, "The Gospel According to St. John: Exposition," *The Interpreter's Bible*, ed. George A. Buttrick, 12 vols. (New York: Abingdon, 1951-57), 8:509.

8. McCartney, pp. 4-5, almost an exact quote from Boreham, p. 252.

9. From Norman Goodall, *One Man's Testimony*, cited by Gerald Kennedy, *A Reader's Notebook* (New York: Harper & Brothers, 1953), p. 167, entry 619.

10. Charles Wesley, "Love Divine, All Loves Excelling," stanza 4.

11. Reported regarding Dr. Lee Shane of the National Baptist Memorial Church, Washington, DC, in *Christianity Today*, July 3, 1961, p. 27. The most representative encyclopedia of preaching, *20 Centuries of Great Preaching* (Waco: Word, 1971), a thirteen-volume collection edited by Clyde E. Fant, Jr., and William M. Pinson, Jr., includes only two sermons on selected aspects of John 3:16: Charles G. Finney's "God's Love For a Sinning World," 3:330-341, and Billy Graham's "Why God Allows Suffering and War," 12:312-320.

12. Maxwell Droke, ed., *The Christian Leader's Golden Treasury* (Indianapolis: Droke House, 1955), p. 363, quoting James Ramsey Ullman in *True*, source undocumented. The quote has become a commonplace. See, for example, Leland Stowe, "The Awesome Challenge of Mt. Aconcague," *The Reader's Digest*, March, 1964, p. 111.

13. Markus Barth, *Ephesians* (Garden City: Doubleday, 1974), 1:397, follows Feuillet in rooting the four-dimensional description of divine reality in the Old Testament wisdom literature. In addition to Job 11:7-9, see also Job 28:12-18; Amos 9:2-3; Psalm 139:7-12; Isaiah 7:10-11.

14. Francis W. Beare, "The Epistle to the Ephesians: Introduction and Exegesis," *The Interpreter's Bible*, ed. George A. Buttrick, 12 vols. (New York: Abingdon, 1951-57), 10:679.

15. For a development of this theme see the sermon by David H. C. Read, "Rooted in the Faith: Roaming in the World," *Virginia Seminary Journal*, November, 1974, pp.

16-17. Read not only develops each dimension along the lines hinted here but also plays upon the subtle dialectic between being rooted and grounded in love (v. 17) and being liberated by love to experience its fullness (vv. 18-19). "It is precisely when the roots are deep and the foundations firm that we are set free to explore and enjoy the infinite dimensions of God's mysterious universe" (p. 16).

16. Note, for example, the study of John by Percy Gardner entitled *The Ephesian Gospel* (New York: G. P. Putnam's Sons, 1915). On the setting of the Fourth Gospel in Ephesus, and its possible connections with the Epistle to the Ephesians, see William E. Hull, "John," *The Broadman Bible Commentary*, ed. Clifton J. Allen, 12 vols. (Nashville: Broadman, 1969-1972), 9:191,199.

17. This correlation between Ephesians 3:18 and John 3:16 was first suggested to me by McCartney, pp. 5-8. Perhaps the best-known such sermon approaching the two texts in this fashion is by W. M. Clow, *The Cross in Christian Experience* (New York: George H. Doran, 1914), pp. 52-64. Note, for example, the summary in *Christianity Today*, October 11, 1963, pp. 54-55.

II
The Breadth of
God's Love

The apostle Paul bids us begin our quest for comprehension by considering the "breadth" of God's love (Eph. 3:18). Thus we interrogate our key verse: "Tell us, precious text, how broad is God's love?" And John 3:16 answers back, "For God so loved *the world* . . . ." In a word, the reach of God's heart is as wide as the universe!

1

At first sight, the affirmation that "God loves the world" seems commonplace indeed, a truism learned in childhood. But on closer inspection we discover that this declaration sets God's love in sharp contrast with our own. For human love is invariably selective, highly discriminating, limited only to a favored few. Stated negatively, if there is anything that we do *not* love, it is "the world" as a whole.

This is true whether we look at the world from a perspective of goodness or of evil. The reformer Martin Luther once cried in characteristically exaggerated fashion, "If I were as our Lord God . . . and these vile people were as disobedient as they now be, I would knock the world in pieces."[1] From the other extreme, Carl Panzram, when he was about to be executed as a criminal in 1930, muttered, "I wish the whole human race had one neck and I had my hands around it."[2]

Strange as it may seem, human love can become so selective that it causes us to hate whatever falls outside a charmed circle. How many times have we been tempted to say with Omar Khayyám:

> Ah, Love! could you and I with Him conspire
> To grasp this sorry Scheme of Things entire,
> Would not we shatter it to bits — and then
> Re-mould it nearer to the Heart's desire![3]

One other poem defines the question forced upon us by this first affirmation of our text.

> If I were God
> And man made a mire
> Of things: war, hatred,
> Murder, lust, cobwebs,
> Of infamy, entangling
> The heart and soul
> I would sweep him
> To one side and start anew.
> (I think I would.)
> If I did this,
> Would I be God?[4]

The resounding answer of John 3:16 is *no*, you would not be God. For this verse affirms without equivocation that God looked at "this sorry Scheme of Things" and loved it every bit! Incredible as it may seem, our foolish, blundering world with all its failings is the recipient of God's unstinting love.

And that is precisely what makes divine love so different from human love. The late Haverford College professor Rufus Jones used to charm audiences by defining his Quakerism as "belief in the fatherhood of God, the brotherhood of man, and the neighborhood of Philadelphia."[5] But God's love is limited to no neighborhood. It plays no favorites. It knows no outsiders. Instead, it leaps over every barrier to embrace persons simply because they are a member of the human race.

To understand the distinctive nature of God's love, we need to clarify the different connotations in three of the most basic words for *love* used at the time when our New Testament was written:[6]

(1) *Eros* is the kind of love elicited because the object is lovely. It roots in our innate desire to possess that which is attractive. Because such English words as *erotic* are based on this Greek term, we may too quickly assume that *eros* is a debased form of exploitative love. Actually, however, it may be a very refined form of the aesthetic impulse that causes us to admire any beautiful work of art. There is nothing intrinsically wrong with "loving" a person because he is physically or psychologically or intellectually attractive, but that is not, and could not be, the kind of love with which God loved our wayward world.

(2) *Philos* is the kind of love based on mutuality between persons. It is a bond forged by common interests with our own kind. This could be patriotic love shared by citizens of the same nation, fraternal love shared by initiates of the same order, or family love shared by members of the same clan. To re-

member the whimsical jest of Rufus Jones, "*Phil*-adelphia" is a compound word meaning city of "brotherly *love*." Again, this is certainly not an inferior type of love, being used of the perfect relationship between Jesus and his Father precisely because they had everything in common (John 5:20). But it could not describe God's love for the world since there is scarcely any mutuality between the two.

(3) *Agape* is the kind of love that is based, not on the nature of the object as lovely, nor on the subject and object as similar, but on the determination of the subject to be loving. It springs from a deliberate intention to do good to others at whatever cost, regardless of their circumstance. Such love is not so much emotional as volitional, not so much sentimental as practical, not so much rooted in the needs of the one loving as in the needs of the one being loved. Quite obviously *agape* is different from either *eros* or *philos*, being especially suited to loving both the unlovely and the unlike — which is exactly the situation which God faced when he acted to love his world!

Summaries are always oversimplified, but it may help to characterize *eros* as sensual love, *philos* as social love, and *agape* as sacrificial love. Another way of expressing the same distinctions is to say that the desire of *eros* is to take, of *philos* is to share, and of *agape* is to give.[7] To be sure, these differences are not consciously pressed in every use of these words, but we may be sensitive to such connotations when the words are employed in a careful theological affirmation such as John 3:16.

It should come as no surprise that the Fourth

Evangelist has chosen the verb for *agape*-love and placed it in a dominant position at the outset of our text. It is his first use of *agapaō*, a verb he will employ thirty-six times, more than twice the number of times it is used in any other book in the New Testament, except the companion epistle, 1 John. The use of this verb here in the aorist indicative form suggests that God's love is not some metaphysical attribute to be contemplated philosophically but is a happening in our history, a once-for-all *act* of God on our behalf to be comprehended existentially.[8] It is not enough to say that "God *is* love" as a timeless proposition. Rather, we must complete that verse by adding that "his love was *disclosed* to us in this, that he *sent* his only Son into the world to bring us life" (1 John 4:9, AT).

In the Greek word order of John 3:16, the verb for *agape*-love is immediately followed by the subject "God" used with a definite article. This grammatical construction reinforces the sense of uniqueness which adheres to God's deed of divine love. We might paraphrase: "The one who has loved in *agape*-fashion is none other than God himself! It was precisely in his role as God that he so loved, and not because he condescended temporarily to function in human fashion. His mercy in loving the world was a direct expression of his majesty as transcendent over the world."[9]

Nowhere is the radical nature of *agape*-love more obvious than in the affirmation of John 3:16 that it was directed to the "world" (Greek: *kosmos*). For this term is not a designation of neutral space, as if to say only that God loved his whole creation (for which

see Matt. 5:45). Rather, the "world," as John 3:16
itself makes clear, is a place of "perishing," a realm
of corruption, dissolution, and death. It is hostile ter-
ritory organized in rebellion against God (see 1 John
2:15-17). There is within the world no attraction
which elicits *eros*-love, or any affinity which elicits
philos-love; instead, there is only antagonism which
elicts *agape*-love.

The notion that God would directly involve himself with such a scene was utterly scandalous to the
Greek mind. The higher religions of Hellenism completely divorced deity from any contact with human
misery. The Stoics thought of God in terms of *apath-
eia*, meaning "incapacity to feel" (from which we get
our English word *apathy*). They reasoned that if God
could be moved by our joy or grief, that would mean
that we could influence him and, therefore, in that
sense, be greater than he. Their only solution was to
remove God from any feeling for this world at all.
Similarly, the Epicureans thought of God in terms of
an undisturbed serenity which required complete
detachment from the world.[10] By contrast, John
dared to declare that *God is vulnerable*, that he committed himself to intervene in humanity's vast hurt.

This shocking affirmation represented a giant
step beyond not only Greek religion but Jewish religion as well. There is no comparable passage in all of
Jewish literature where God is said to "love the
world" in such indiscriminate fashion. Instead, the
characteristic emphasis is on his love for Israel (a climactic expression of which is found in Hos. 11:1-11).
But what in the Old Testament was seen primarily
as *covenant*-love (Hebrew *hesed*) is here seen as *cos-*

mic-love (Greek *agape*), not in order to abrogate
God's earlier covenants with Israel but in order to
universalize and thereby fulfill them. No longer is
God's special favor thought to be focused on a particular people. Instead, *agape* has been made the ultimate basis for defining Christianity as a religion of
"world" redemption without regard to ancestry, nationality, or culture. What this means is that our
faith exists not to preserve certain ethnic traditions,
or to serve as the cement for Western civilization,
but to express the unqualified concern of God for
every person on the face of this earth regardless of
human qualifications.

2

The consequences of this world-embracing *agape*
are both vertical and horizontal. That is, the truth
that God loves the world transforms the very nature
of our relationship both to God and to all of humanity. Here we will deal with the spiritual implications
of this affirmation, leaving the ethical implications
for the concluding section of this chapter.

What is at stake spiritually in the affirmation that
"God loved the world" is nothing less than the nature of ultimate reality. Is our world finally a cold,
impersonal machine with no meaning or feeling at
its core? As Walter de la Mare's poem, "The Listeners," asked: "Is there anybody there?" said the
Traveller,/Knocking on the moonlit door ..."[11]

That question once seemed easy to answer when
the edge of our world appeared no farther away than
the fleecy clouds. Thomas Hood has captured the

nostalgia of our spiritual childhood with its scientific innocence:

> I remember, I remember
> The fir-trees dark and high;
> I used to think their slender tops
> Were close against the sky:
> It was a childish ignorance,
> But now 'tis little joy
> To know I'm farther off from Heaven
> Than when I was a boy.[12]

In place of the intimate, lively little world of the first century, our universe seems to have become an unbending cage of mathematical rigidity. The Russian cosmonauts who thrust themselves beyond our farthest cloud assured us that they found no God "out there." As our space probes have carried us deeper and deeper into a planetary wilderness devoid of life, gradually "the horror of vastness" has come upon us, and we shudder with a cosmic chill.

Arthur Koestler has written movingly of man's expulsion from his cozy world to live under sentence of exile in a prison house of infinity.

> The Aristotelian universe was centralised.
> ... The Copernican Universe is ... *decentralized*, perplexing, anarchic. It has no natural centre of orientation to which everything else can be referred. ... The notion of limitlessness or infinity, which the Copernican system implied, was bound to devour the space reserved for God ... This meant, among other things, the end of intimacy between God and man. *Homo sapiens* had dwelt

in a universe enveloped by divinity as by a womb; now he was being expelled from the womb.[13]

Our space explosion raises with new urgency the age-old question, "Is this a friendly universe?"[14] No longer are we able to live in a geocentric universe, which put our earth at the center of everything, or even a heliocentric universe, in which our earth was centered around the sun. Now, instead, we must inhabit a galactocentric universe which "put the earth and its life near the edge of one great galaxy in a universe of millions of galaxies. Man becomes peripheral among the billions of stars of his own Milky Way; and, according to the revelations of paleontology and geochemistry, he is recent and apparently ephemeral in the unrolling of cosmic time."[15]
Are we, then, as one of Galsworthy's characters has it, just "a gnat for all of that," no more than specks on the side of a spinning ball orbiting endlessly in one corner of trackless space? As our cosmos grows infinitely more complex, is it still realistic to affirm that "God so loved the *kosmos*...?" In other words, does John 3:16 presuppose such a hopelessly outdated cosmology that its fundamental premise is now obsolete?
In answering that crucial question we need to remember that in the first century, as the Christian message moved from its Jewish cradle in Palestine to the sophisticated centers of the Greco-Roman world, it early encountered a Gnostic mentality which viewed the universe as a vast prison whose innermost dungeon was earth. Space itself was con-

ceived of as successive spheres that tyrannized man, suffocating his every effort to hold communion with the divine. Between earth and heaven were layers of space populated by aeons or demiurges personifying the cosmic terror that held man trapped in an alien realm of darkness, unable to reach the realm of light.[16]

As best we can tell, this pervasive Gnostic mentality was especially strong in Asia Minor, forcing Paul to recast his message as we know it from Galatians and Romans into an entirely new form as we know it from Colossians and Ephesians. It is quite possible that his deliberate use of four dimensions in Ephesians 3:18 was intended to refute the Gnostic notion that the outer reaches of space were in themselves demonic.[17] No, countered the apostle, go as far as possible in any direction imaginable, and you will discover that the entire universe is permeated not with a hostile darkness but with a divine love such as was seen in the solitary life of Jesus Christ (see Rom. 8:39).

Writing in the same milieu of Gnostic fatalism, the author of the Ephesian Gospel of John flung back the answer of the Christian faith to those in any generation who succumb to the sinisterness of space: God has not forsaken or abandoned this world of ours but has loved and affirmed it in Jesus Christ our Lord! As a philosophy of existence this means that the arms of the universe are extended not to crush but to embrace. Life is not out to "get" us, to thwart or to mock us, but to woo and to win us. The primary datum with which our faith begins is this: *You are loved* simply because you are a child of the universe!

This means that the gospel always begins, not with the subjective question, "Do you happen to love God?" but with the objective declaration, "God most assuredly loves you!" As 1 John put it, "In this is love, *not* that we loved God but that *he loved us*" (1 John 4:10, RSV, author's italics). Stated baldly, we must all face the fact that we are already loved by God whether we happen to like it or not! To be sure, this divine initiative demands a human response, but the decision whether to love back in return may be made in the confidence that God is *for us* rather than against us (see Rom. 8:31).

One of my most memorable introductions to this truth came when I served as pastor of a couple who, after eleven years of marriage, had been blessed with ten children — none of them twins! On one occasion, when the eldest was fourteen and the youngest was three, I discussed with the mother some of the difficulties of managing such a brood, questioning whether some of her children were ever neglected, unnoticed, or accidentally left behind. Her reply: "No, I never forget a one of them, 'cause they're all precious to me."

I learned an important lesson that day: love does not work by the law of division — one mother's heart divided into ten small parts and parceled out to each child. Rather, love works by the law of multiplication — one mother's heart multiplied tenfold, so that each child had as much love as if he or she were the only child! No wonder Victor Hugo exclaimed, "Mother love: that magic which multiplies as it is divided."[18]

Multiply that mother love by infinity and you begin to get an intimation of eternity. Even with a

population explosion that now numbers humanity in
the teeming billions, John 3:16 is the gospel's way of
letting God say to all who will listen, "I never miss a
one of you, 'cause you're all precious to me!" Or, as
Augustine put it centuries ago, "God loves each one
of us as if there was only one of us to love."[19]

3

One of the great dangers in attempting a balanced
statement of the gospel is that of divorcing evan-
gelism from ethics, thereby driving a cleft between
our relationship to God and our responsibility to
humankind. This hiatus between doctrine and duty
is a particular temptation when talking about love
because of the sentimental connotations of the word
in popular culture. Indeed, some theologians are
wary of rooting the gospel in the love of God for fear
that its more astringent demands be dissolved into a
mushy religious romanticism.

But if we press the inescapable implications of the
simple affirmation with which John 3:16 begins, we
discover that a profound unity between personal
conversion and social concern is rooted precisely in
the fact that God loves the world. For if this be true,
it means, not only that God loves me prior to and
apart from my love for him, but that God loves
every one of my neighbors before I decide whether I
shall love them or not. We saw in the previous section that the Gospel does not begin with our subjective feelings, that is "Do you happen to love God?"
but with the objective fact that God most certainly
loves us. Now we see that Christian ethics is rooted,

not in human attitudes, that is, "Do you happen to love your neighbors?" but in the divine announcement that God already loves each and every one of them!

If God really does love "*the world*," this confronts us with the uncomfortable fact that he has already acted to love those whom our inherited prejudices and social environment may have conditioned us to despise. We may have been reared to look down on "foreigners" as immigrants with unpronounceable names, or to hate the Germans or Japanese as our nation's enemies in World War II, or to ridicule certain minorities as menial laborers without any culture.

If so, John 3:16 suddenly exposes an unbearable discrepancy between our attitudes and those of almighty God! The very people we have almost unconsciously come to view with contempt he has already decided to adore with an everlasting love. Even if we harbor no covert animosities, still our whole social orientation is called into question by John 3:16 because it discloses the costly compassion of God for those whom we may be treating with benign neglect.

This profound disparity between the lavishness of God's love and the stinginess of our own is at once a judgment that condemns and a grace that heals. For to say that God loves the world also means that his love is a "given" interposed between us and every potential relationship into which we may enter. Obviously, no person can have contact with the vast majority of those who share the same time and space on planet Earth. But no matter who we meet, how-

ever chance the encounter, the first and foremost
consideration shaping our response should be the
realization that this is a person *already loved by God*!
This "given" delivers us from the tyranny of having
to think first about the person's color or nationality
or education or economic standing. A revolution in
human relationships stems from this incredible possibility of viewing persons not in accordance with
their social status but in accordance with their
standing as divinely beloved.

We are now in a position to unite the fact that God
loves every one of us with the twin fact that he loves
every one of our neighbors. Jesus was the first to
combine the two into a "new commandment":
"Love one another; even as I have loved you" (John
13:34, RSV). The newness of this commandment
consists in the way that it transcends "the great
commandment in the law," namely, to "love your
neighbor as yourself" (Matt. 22:36,39, RSV). The
Old Testament approach was to base love for others
on the command that we love God, whereas the New
Testament approach was to base it on the way in
which God has already loved us. The Old Testament
norm for neighbor-love was self-love, that is, you
should love others as you would wish them to love
you back in return (see Matt. 7:12). The New Testament norm for neighbor-love was Christ-love, that
is, you should love others as Christ loved those who
were about to deny him (John 13:38) by laying down
his life on their behalf. The difference is decisive, for
Christ did not love others as he loved himself.
Rather, he loved them *far more* than he loved himself! (see John 13:1).

The New Testament is very realistic about our inability to love as we should. Therefore, it not only
holds up the love of Christ as a new norm but actually suggests that such love is lavished on us through
the gift of the Holy Spirit to our hearts (Rom. 5:5). In
other words, we are not bidden to mount a maximum
effort in wrenching from human love more than it is
capable of providing. Rather, we are bidden to love
others with God's own love that grows in our hearts
as "the fruit of the Spirit" (Gal. 5:22, RSV). Dietrich
Bonhoeffer has well described the intercessory role
of such love:

> We are separated from one another by an un-
> bridgeable gulf of otherness and strangeness
> which resists all our attempts to overcome it
> by means of natural association or emotional
> or spiritual union. There is no way from one
> person to another. However loving and sym-
> pathetic we try to be, however sound our
> psychology, however frank and open our be-
> havior, we cannot penetrate the incognito of
> the other man, for there are no direct rela-
> tionships, not even between soul and soul.
> Christ stands between us, and we can only
> get into touch with our neighbors through
> him.[20]

While living for a year on sabbatical leave with
Dietrich Bonhoeffer's twin sister, Sabine, and her
husband, Gerhard Leibholz, at the University of
Goettingen, Germany, I learned a beautiful illustra-
tion of this Christocentric love from their domestic
servant, Frau Anna Henke. In the depth of World

War II, food was so severely rationed that Frau
Henke saved for months to get enough sugar and
other ingredients to bake a tiny birthday cake for
her aged mother. On the appointed day she went to
the railway station to catch a train that would take
her, and that precious cake, to her mother in a
nearby rural village. But as she waited in the station,
her eyes fell upon a Polish mother with her baby,
both of them emaciated to the point of starvation.
For generations, bitter hostility had festered between Germans and Poles, causing the Nazi govern-
ment to deprive its Polish citizens, even more than
its German citizens, of the basic necessities of life.

Moved by the sight of such desperate hunger,
Frau Henke quietly laid her little cake in the baby
carriage when the mother was not looking and then
prepared to board her train empty-handed. But the
Dresden railway station was teeming with Gestapo
agents during the war, and one of them, seeing what
she had done, stepped forward to ask reproachfully
why she, a German, would do such a thing for a Pole.
With quiet courage, that simple servant woman
turned to the dreaded Gestapo agent and responded,
"I did not give it to her as a German to a Pole but as a
Christian to one of Christ's own!"

Despite the most insidious propaganda demeaning
Poles, despite the danger raised by mere suspicion
during that reign of terror, despite the poignant desire to present her aging mother with one more
birthday cake, Frau Henke had learned the incredible truth that awaits our discovery from John 3:16.
Because God loved the world, we never meet a person whom he does not give us the capacity to love
even as he first loved him in Jesus Christ, our Lord!

Notes

1. Martin Luther, *Table Talk*, III, cited by Arthur John Gossip, "The Gospel According to St. John: Exposition," *The Interpreter's Bible*, ed. by George A. Buttrick, 12 vols. (New York: Abingdon, 1951-57), 8:510.

2. Pen-ultimate, "The Shape of the Week," *The Christian Century*, November 1, 1961, p. 1319, quoting from Barnaby Conrad, *Famous Last Words* (Garden City: Doubleday, 1961).

3. Edward FitzGerald, *The Rubáiyát of Omar Khayyám* (David McKay, 1942), stanza 99.

4. Maxwell Droke, ed., *The Christian Leader's Golden Treasury* (Indianapolis: Droke House, 1955), p. 218, from *The Evangelical Beacon.*

5. "Personal Glimpses," *The Reader's Digest*, May, 1976, p. 72, from Robert Fuoss in *Dynamic Maturity.*

6. The classic study in modern theology is Anders Nygren, *Agape and Eros* (London: S.P.C.K., 1954), esp. pp. 28-48, 61-159. Despite the great influence of this work, it is now generally agreed that some of the conclusions are overdrawn and need to be balanced by more recent studies in theological lexicography. For a brief summary on "New Testament Words for Love," with references to most relevant bibliography in the footnotes, see Victor Paul Furnish, *The Love Command in the New Testament* (Nashville: Abingdon, 1972), pp. 219-231.

7. These categories were suggested by Archibald M. Hunter, *Interpreting Paul's Gospel* (Philadelphia: Westminster, 1955), p. 47, who quotes G. B. Caird as follows: "*Eros* is all take; *philia* is give and take; *agapē* is all give."

8. John Marsh, *The Gospel of St. John* (Baltimore: Penguin, 1968), p. 183.

9. Ceslaus Spicq, *Agape in the New Testament* (St. Louis: B. Herder, 1966), 3:16.

10. William Barclay, "Great Themes of the New Testament," *The Expository Times* 70 (December, 1958):81-82.

11. Walter de la Mare, "The Listeners," stanza 1. Cited in *Masterpieces of Religious Verse*, ed. James Dalton Morrison (New York: Harper & Brothers, 1948), p. 61.

12. Thomas Hood, "I Remember, I Remember," stanza 4. Cited in Morrison, ibid., p. 282. Cf. Alan Richardson, *The Bible in the Age of Science* (Philadelphia: Westminster, 1961), p. 165.

13. Arthur Koestler, *The Sleepwalkers* (London: Hutchinson, 1959), p. 218.

14. I remember reading somewhere that the philosopher Lessing once remarked that if he had but one question to ask the Sphinx it would be, "Is this a friendly universe?" but I cannot now locate the source. The question is attributed to F. W. H. Myers by George A. Buttrick, "The Gospel According to Matthew: Exposition," *The Interpreter's Bible*, ed. George A. Buttrick, 12 vols. (New York: Abingdon, 1951-57), 8:341.

15. Harlow Shapley, "Man's Fourth Adjustment," *The American Scholar* 25 (1956):454.

16. Hans Jonas, *The Gnostic Religion* (Boston: Beacon, 1958), pp. 48-74.

17. Georg Bertram, "*hupsos*," *Theological Dictionary of the New Testament*, ed. Gerhard Friedrich (Grand Rapids: Wm. B. Eerdmans, 1972), 8:604, n. 24.

18. Quoted by memory from a source which I cannot now locate.

19. Cited by William Barclay, *The Gospel of John* (Philadelphia: Westminster, 1958), 1:129.

20. Dietrich Bonhoeffer, *The Cost of Discipleship*, rev. and unabridged edition (New York: Macmillan, 1959), pp. 87-88.

III
The Length of God's Love

A sinister note emerged in our study of the first dimension of God's love which we must now consider more directly. Tracing the breadth of God's love, we discovered that he loved a world that did not love him back in return. As the immediate context of John 3:16 makes clear, the God of light (John 1:5; 1 John 1:5) lavished his affections on a world that "loved darkness rather than light" (John 3:19, KJV).

The most painful experience in life is to offer love that is not reciprocated. C. S. Lewis noted: "To love at all is to be vulnerable. Love anything, and your heart will certainly be wrung and possibly be broken."[1] Young people searching for love worthy of a lifetime commitment often discover the heartbreak of proffering affections that are rebuffed by indifference. Some parents experience the excruciating agony of loving their children from birth only to have them spurn that love for no apparent reason in later adolescence.

God's love for the world was met with outright rejection, thus raising the problem of divine pain. The Tzeltal Indians of Chiapas in southern Mexico have a word for love which means "to hurt in the heart."

Therefore, their translation of John 3:16 captures
some of the pathos of the point which we are making
here in its rendition, "God so hurt in his heart that
he ..."[2] That he what? Using the categories of
Paul's four dimensions we are ready to ask, To what
length did God go to love a world that would not love
him back in return? John 3:16 makes ready answer:
"he gave his only Son" (RSV).

1

The little word *so*, which stands first in the original Greek text of our key verse, both anticipates the
magnitude of God's response and affirms that it is
commensurate with the magnitude of the problem
being addressed. The grammatical construction
(*houtōs ... hōste*) is unusual, stressing that the coming of Christ to earth as an epiphany of God's love
was a direct result of the divine determination to
grapple with its loveless condition. We might paraphrase the force of the connection between the first
two phrases in John 3:16 as follows: "God loved the
world so much that he actually gave his only Son as
tangible proof of just how great that love really
was."[3] John McIntyre has expressed it more precisely:

> For so compassionately and understandingly
> was God concerned about the world, that He
> loved up to the point of giving His own Son;
> so concerned was He to invest with value hu-
> man existence which had thrown itself away
> in succumbing to temptation, and to restore
> meaning into a situation which was empty to

the point of nihilistic despair, that the gift of
His Son proved the only true measure of His
concern.[4]

In other words, the very construction of John
3:16 establishes a profound connection between loving and giving. God gave, not because of any human
coercion or entreaty, but only because he loved. Indeed, to love the world meant inevitably to give to
the world, because God's kind of love always ex-
presses itself in giving. It is as much the nature of
agape to give as it is the nature of fire to burn or the
nature of light to shine. As we saw in Chapter II,
that is precisely what sets it apart from human love,
which is so often a matter of getting rather than of
giving. Frequently, the romantic "I love you" really
means "I love me and I want you" in a clutching,
possessive sense.

There is no external compulsion in God's love. It
arises spontaneously out of the divine initiative as a
free gift. These are the terms in which Jesus under-
stood his earthly destiny: "For this reason the
Father *loves* me, because I lay down my life, that I
may take it again. *No one takes it from me*, but I lay
it down of my own accord" (John 10:17-18, author's
italics). The verb used in John 3:16 for "gave"
(*edōken*) often means "to give a present." When God
gave Jesus to the world, it was his way of saying, "I
love you so much that I have a present for you."[5]
There is no hint here of constraint or reluctance, as
if God begrudgingly allowed his Son to leave heaven
as a last resort.

That sheer spontaneity in giving does not mean,

however, that it was easy for God to part with his gift. To begin with, the aorist form of the verb "gave" underscores the realism of the relinquishment. A day came when the deed was done, when the Son was gone, when the Father's bosom was empty (John 1:18), when eternity had voluntarily yielded to the needs of time. Moreover, there is an unmistakable suggestion of sacrifice in God's sending of his Son to love a loveless world. That is why Moffatt translates, "God loved the world so dearly that he *gave up* his only Son ..." (author's italics, also see Rom. 8:32).[6] For when a present is given "with no strings attached," it becomes vulnerable to the whims of the recipient, as when a thoughtless child smashes a valuable gift provided by loving parents. An infinitely greater risk was inherent in the giving of God's Son to a world confused enough to love darkness rather than light.

In the Catskill Mountains near Kingston, New York, a road winds along the hillside bordering a lovely lake. As one looks down upon the crystal waters, ringed with wooded forests unmolested by commercial enterprises, it seems a shame that such beauty is denied to human use. But near a spot where many stop to savor the scene is a neatly-lettered sign, "Ashokan Reservoir—New York City Water Supply." Suddenly the realization dawns that all of this freshness and purity is not denied mankind, for its real destination is ninety miles down the valley where it emerges from a long aqueduct to wash away the stain of a great city.[7]

Just so, God's love is not locked in the heavens, inaccessible to human need. Instead, in the gift of

Jesus Christ, God's love ran down the infinitely long aqueduct between eternity and time. The incarnation meant that heavenly love suddenly gushed forth on earth to cleanse its stains of sin and sorrow. When the everlasting mercy grew hands and feet and face and "dwelt among us," it was as if a heavenly reservoir of love had been emptied on our behalf. To be sure, that crystal fountain could not remain unsullied on these earthly shores, but it is the proper business of love to get itself dirty with the plight of mankind.

2

A further indication of the length to which God's love would go is provided by the description of his gift as "the Son" (*ton huion*). We need not enter here into the thicket of Trinitarian theology in order to grasp the implications of this designation. Perhaps a simple analogy will suffice.

I happen to have one son. If we were being compared, two distinctions would be crucial to a balanced understanding of our relationship. On the one hand, it could be said that we are certainly *not* the same. I shall always be his father, and he will always be my son. Our roles, in other words, are not reversible. We are two persons, each with a distinct identity in relation both to one another and to others. On the other hand, it could also be said that we *are* the same. For although my son is not me, he is the very extension of my life, bone of my bone and flesh of my flesh. We share not only common genetic material but an intimacy of spirit unique to father and son. It is fair to say that I relate to my son as to none other. Even though I love many persons very dearly, there is a special quality to the love for my son because he is my very own.

In like manner, we may make two similar statements about the relationship between God and Jesus. To begin with, they were clearly *not* the same, for the Son went forth from the Father and depended entirely upon him (John 5:19). Heaven was not empty when Jesus walked upon earth. Jesus was not talking to himself when he prayed to the Father. For here were two different persons whose relationship to each other never changed. At the same time, to say that Jesus was not God devalues the significance of his life. For, in an equally true sense, he *was* God, the very extension of God's life into the world of darkness. As "the Son," he was spirit of God's spirit, purpose of God's purpose, love of God's love. The old adage, "Like father, like son," suggests that, in sending one who was Son, the heavenly Father involved his very being in our human predicament.

It is in the Prologue to the Fourth Gospel (John 1:1-18) that the Father-Son relationship is most carefully elaborated. The passage begins with the quite different analogy of the speaker and his word in order to make the point that a person's thoughts are a part of his nature and yet they can go forth from him when expressed in words. Just so, Jesus was God's self-disclosure in a "word made flesh" (v. 14, AT). But by the end of the passage, the analogy has shifted from the "Word with God" (v. 1, AT) to the "Son in the bosom of the Father" (v. 18, AT). Why this sudden shift that at first seems to change the point of the passage? Because it declares the content of the supreme "word" that Jesus brought to earth: God is not a theoretical concept to be pondered but a loving Father with a Son clasped to his bosom!

This introduction of family language into the heart of our text further underscores the costliness of divine love. Sir Harry Lauder was once told of a little boy who went walking with his father at sunset during World War I when it was customary for families to hang a service flag in the window. Noticing such banners with one or more stars at their center, the child inquired and his father explained that each star represented a son from that home in the service of his country. When they came to a break in the houses, they could see through the gap the evening star shining brightly in the sky. Tugging at his father's hand once more, the child exclaimed, "Oh, look, Daddy, God must have given *His* Son, for He has got a star in *His* window."[8]

And so it is, for in the warfare of light with darkness, God decided to volunteer his most precious family member for service in the fray. The tragic consequences of that commitment we shall seek to trace in the next chapter. For now, it is enough to note that, by placing no restrictions on the gift, God allowed even his Son to become a casualty on our behalf.

3

A final factor in comprehending the length to which God would go in loving the world is indicated

by the description of his Son as "only" (RSV) or
"only begotten" (KJV). Because our best-known
translations differ significantly in rendering this
term, we shall need to turn aside long enough to
clear up the resulting confusion.[9]

The conflicting translations are all efforts to ren-
der the Greek adjective *monogenēs*, a compound
from *monos*, meaning "only" or "alone" (compare
the English word *monotone*), and *genos* meaning
"kind" or "class" (compare the English word *genus*).
In combination, the parts mean literally "only one of
a kind" or "unique." The familiar KJV translation
"only *begotten*" (author's italics) came into English
not from the original Greek but from the later Latin
version of Jerome who, for dogmatic reasons,
changed the Latin *unicus* ("only") to *unigenitus*
("only begotten") in John 3:16. Even though William Tyndale, the first translator of the New Testament from Greek to English in 1534, avoided Jerome's mistake ("he hath geven his only sonne"), it
was repeated in most other translations until the
twentieth century because of the great influence
both of the Vulgate as the official Bible of the
Roman Catholic Church and of the King James Version as the most popular "authorized" edition in
Protestantism.

With a bit of thought we can see why John, of all
New Testament books, would not speak of Jesus as
"only *begotten*." For the word "beget" implies
birth, or a coming-into-being, whereas the Fourth
Gospel is our clearest witness to the eternal preexis-
tence of God's Son (John 1:1; 8:58; 17:24). According
to the Evangelist, it is incorrect to imply that there

was ever a time when the Son did not exist. Some theologians in the early church tried to have it both ways by speaking of the "eternal generation" of the Son, but of this overly-subtle and unnecessary paradox our Gospel knows nothing. Therefore, the dropping of the KJV word *begotten* in the RSV translation of John 3:16 was done in the interest of accuracy and in no way throws doubt on either the supernatural birth or the full deity of Christ.

There is one passage in the New Testament which not only confirms our clarification of *monogenēs* but points us toward some of the richer aspects of its meaning. In Hebrews 11:17 (AT), it is said that Abraham "was ready to offer up his only (*monogenē*) son," Isaac. Obviously, the meaning cannot be that Isaac was the only son ever begotten by Abraham, for Ishmael was well known as another son born thirteen years earlier (Gen. 16:1-4,15; 17:1,15-16,25). The point must be, rather, that Isaac was the only son of promise, the unique channel through which Abraham's descendants would be blessed.

Even more important in Hebrews 11:17 is the reference to the story in Genesis 22:1-19, where Isaac is three times called Abraham's "only" son (vv. 2,12,16). There, in a context of impending sacrifice, the connotation of "only" is clearly that of a son who is uniquely beloved. "Take your son, your *only* son Isaac, *whom you love* ... and offer him" (Gen. 22:2 RSV, author's italics). In a careful study of the Greek word for *beloved* (*agapētos*), with which God affirmed his Son at the baptism and transfiguration of Jesus (Mark 1:11; 9:7), C. H. Turner has shown that the meaning is virtually identical to that of *mon-ogenēs* (Latin *unicus*) and thus should be rendered "only" in the same sense that we have just found in Genesis 22.[10] Hints of an Isaac typology lurk in the very language of John 3:16 with the decisive difference that God gave up freely the one thing that he would not take from Abraham, his only beloved son.[11]

With this factual information in hand, we are ready to feel the emotional impact of the assertion that the Son whom God gave out of love for the world was the "only" Son that he had ever loved like that. At first glance, it seems incredible that God sent just one Son to deal with a whole universe of darkness. But now we begin to understand that the magnitude of the gift matched the magnitude of the need.[12] One living person pitted against millions of loveless hearts—yet the two were commensurate. For love can only happen in one life at a time, and all the love that God had to offer was compressed into that one solitary life. *God loved all there was to love by giving all there was to give!*

There is a chilling singularity to that word *only* for, historically, it stands in contrast with the many others whom God had used to do his bidding. It is almost as if God surveyed all of the lawgivers, kings, priests, prophets, and seers of the Old Testament and concluded, "Not enough." All of the angels and archangels, cherubim and seraphim of heaven, but, still, "Not enough." At last, his eye fell on his Son, the one with whom he enjoyed the most intimate fellowship imaginable. And God said, "Finally, I have found the perfect gift. Because I love my Son uniquely, in giving him up the world will at last realize that I love it uniquely as well!"

Forget the notion that this Son was "only *begotten*"—there are no maternity wards in heaven! Remember, instead, that he was "only *beloved*"— that Christ was in a class by himself as the recipient of God's love. If, then, that Son was sent into our world, he carried with him the reality of that overwhelming devotion of a Father who was "well pleased" with all that he ever did (see Mark 1:11, KJV). Jesus could love us extravagantly because he had already been loved extravagantly himself from all eternity. Now, God had an ultimate stake in what would become of our sorry lot, not just because he had made us but because his "only beloved" had forever become a part of us.

One afternoon the actor, Charles Laughton, went to a hospital to read to a small group of nonambulatory patients. Among them was a tiny figure of a lady in a wheelchair who had been a nurse in World War I and had lived in the hospital ever since. She had suffered shell shock in a heavy artillery battle and never recovered from the experience. When Laughton finished reading he asked her name, since her face had been particularly rapt during his presentation. She replied "Jennie," whereupon the great actor recited Leigh Hunt's "Rondeau," "Jennie kissed me." After a moment the little woman looked up into that famous face recognizable to millions and in a quiet, almost birdlike voice said, "I don't know who you are or where you came from but I love you." The big man moved out of the room quickly before she could see the tears starting to well up in his eyes.[13]

Many a brooding existentialist has likened planet

Earth to an asylum for the shell-shocked victims of life's brutalities. But John 3:16 declares that our little planet has been visited by one who can limn the lines of a Father's love as no one else because he uniquely experienced such love for himself. We did not send for him, nor, to this day, do some recognize him, even though he has now become familiar to millions. But the love which he shares can awaken love within our hearts. Looking up in amazement at the disclosure of such love, our first response need only be to whisper, "I don't know who you are or where you came from but I love you."

Notes

1. C. S. Lewis, *The Four Loves* (New York: Harcourt, Brace & World, 1960), p. 169.

2. "God's Word in Man's Language," *Bible Society Record* 102 (September, 1957):100.

3. On the force of the "*houtōs ... hōste*" construction, see Raymond E. Brown, *The Gospel According to John* (Garden City: Doubleday, 1966), 1:133-134; Leon Morris, *The Gospel According to John* (Grand Rapids: Eerdmans, 1971), p. 229; W. F. Howard, *Christianity According to St. John* (Philadelphia: Westminster, 1946), pp. 62-63; Ceslaus Spicq, *Agape in the New Testament* (St. Louis: B. Herder, 1966), 3:17.

4. John McIntyre, *On the Love of God* (New York: Harper & Brothers, 1962), p. 55.

5. Spicq, 3:17.

6. G. H. C. MacGregor, *The Gospel of John* (New York: Harper & Brothers, 1928), p. 81. Cf. Brown, 1:134; Rudolf Bultmann, *The Gospel of John* (Philadelphia: Westminster, 1971), p. 154, n. 3.

7. Robert E. Luccock, "The Dimensions of God's Love," *If God Be for Us* (New York: Harper & Brothers, 1954), p. 145.

8. F. W. Boreham, *A Handful of Stars* (New York: Abingdon, 1922), pp. 260-61. Told by Sir Harry Lauder in Melbourne, Australia, shortly after his only son had fallen at the front in World War I.

9. For a much more complete discussion of the meaning of *monogenēs* in John 3:16 see, in addition to the commentaries, Dale Moody, "God's Only Son: The Translation of John 3:16 in the Revised Standard Version," *Journal of Biblical Literature* 72 (1953):213-219; F. C. Grant, " 'Only Begotten' — A Footnote to the New Revision," *Anglican Theological Review* 36 (1954):284-287; R. L. Roberts, "The Rendering 'Only Begotten' in John 3:16," *Restoration Quarterly* 16 (1973):2-22.

10. C. H. Turner, "*ho huios mou ho agapētos*," *Journal of Theological Studies* 27 (January, 1926):113-129.

11. H. W. Watkins, *The Gospel According to St. John* (London: Cassell, 1902), pp. 81-82. For further details on the Isaac typology see Brown, 1:147.

12. John Marsh, *The Gospel of St John* (Baltimore: Penguin, 1968), p. 183.

13. Recounted by Ben Irwin, Laughton's public relations representative for some six years before the actor's death in 1962, and reprinted in *The Courier-Journal & Times*, Louisville, Kentucky, December 14, 1969, B-2.

IV
The Depth of God's Love

The farther we journey into John 3:16, the more insistently a dissonant sound is heard. First, we are told that God went out of his way to love a world that preferred to love darkness rather than light. Then, we are told that he handed over the crown jewel of heaven, his only beloved Son, as a concrete demonstration of just how extravagantly he was determined to love earth's wayward rebels. But once we pass the midpoint of our remarkable text, the tragic theme becomes explicit in that somber phrase, "should not *perish*."

The sound of such a harsh word breaks any reverie that might tempt us to sentimentalize John 3:16. A stinkweed grows in our fragrant garden, and we abhor its pungent smell! How could a loving God make any provision for people to perish? Why bring up an idea so awful only to negate it? Indeed, does a word like *perish* ever belong in a sentence on love?

In search of answers we return to Paul's prayer and discover there his insistence that we ponder the "depth" of God's love (Eph. 3:18). When we ask just how deeply God's love would descend, this disturbing phrase in John 3:16 provides the needed insight: It would go where people are perishing! In Jesus

Christ, God not only visited our fickle planet but
threw his arms around every ugly thing that he
found here.[1] Down in the abyss of human existence
where life crumbles apart, the beloved Son grappled
with that self-destruction which we inflict upon ourselves every time we spurn the offer of love.

1

The possibility of perishing is introduced into our
text as the normal, expected, inevitable end of humankind — our certain fate unless something, or
Someone, intervenes. It is not that we possess a
spark of immortality that guarantees survival except for those who stumble into the void. Rather, the
assumption is that we are all headed for eternal ruin
unless it can somehow be averted. This sober assess-
ment is not based on a pessimistic theory of human
nature but on the simple fact of our proclivity for
perdition (John 3:19-20). If at last we are destroyed,
it is not because God made us flawed but because
"our deeds are evil" (v. 19, AT). Nor can this descent
into darkness be blamed on abandonment by God.
John 3:16 is not saying that God gave up on us because he offered a love that was rejected. Rather, it
is saying that God responded to our desperate predicament in love precisely because of that very rejection!
    The verdict that, left to our own devices, we will
eventually self-destruct is harsh but realistic. Although we never like to admit or even discuss such
things, frankly our propensity for perishing is staggering. Think how much of nature we have already

ravished in but a moment of time since the Industrial Revolution. Our streams have become open sewers, our fertile plains turned into dust bowls, our natural resources depleted—all in the name of "civilization." The same sense of exhaustion pervades time as well as space. Viewing the broad sweep of history, Gibbon, Spengler, and Toynbee have all pointed to decline, decay, and even death within whole cultures. It seems that everything we touch is corrupted even when we intend it least.

Most poignant of all is the personal level "when a thing has gone to hell inside you" (to borrow a phrase from D. H. Lawrence). For nothing is quite so destructive to the human heart as to live without love. Without love of country, patriotism perishes. Without love of service, vocations perish. Without love of peace, diplomacy perishes. Without love of family, homes perish. Without love of self, integrity perishes. Without love of neighbor, community perishes. Without love of God, values perish. Leave anything human devoid of love long enough, and it will finally wither and die! Summing up the psychiatric training and counseling experiences of a lifetime, Dr. Smiley Blanton defined the alternatives posed by our text in their simplest terms: *Love or Perish*.[2]

Lacking love, the connective tissues of life are broken, leaving us isolated and lonely, bereft of companionship. The resulting lack of communication breeds suspicion, which in turn feeds cynicism, which finally ends in bitterness and despair. Without love, we lack the confidence to express gratitude or compassion or affection. Gradually, our emotions become cloistered, our imaginations shriveled, our life-styles a drudgery of defensive routine. And underneath it all, there lurks an aching sense of not being needed, of not really mattering to anybody, of having no urgent reason to live.

Bennett Cerf, the publisher at Random House, once appeared on a NBC radio program called "Conversation" when the topic was, "What are you most afraid of?" After the panelists had reached a consensus of "annihilation by the Bomb," moderator Clifton Fadiman noticed that Cerf had not contributed to the vigorous discussion. When prodded, the famous raconteur replied, in a diffident voice, that he had hesitated to answer the question truthfully because his concern would seem trivial beside the vast issues that others had introduced. But then he added that since the point of the program was to share what one really thought, he might as well admit that "what he feared most was not being loved."[3]

While we need not minimize the threat of atomic annihilation, its destruction for many would be mercifully swift, whereas death from not being loved is always slow and painful. No bomb has been invented that can inflict as much cruelty on the vital core of our being as the blight of feeling that no one ever cares. Survivors of a nuclear holocaust could respond to the devastation about them with a courageous determination to rebuild the wreckage, whereas the plague of lovelessness leaves no survivors because the wreckage is all within.

Before we move beyond this diagnosis of our condition, let us note the close connection not only between loving and perishing but also between both of these dialectical realities and the dimension of "depth." When we have no cords of love to tie us to others, we begin to flee. No sooner did Adam choose to forfeit his intimate fellowship with God for a bite of forbidden fruit than he tried to run and hide (Gen. 3:8). Without the constraints of love (2 Cor. 5:14), life becomes a fugitive enterprise, a flight from the emptiness left by spurning love.

Francis Thompson has given classic expression to this futile effort to escape from the claims of love:

> I fled Him, down the nights and down the days;
>   I fled him down the arches of the years;
> I fled him down the labyrinthine ways
>   Of my own mind; and in the mist of tears
> I hid from Him, and under running laughter.
>   Up vistaed hopes I sped;
>   And shot, precipitated,
>   Adown titanic glooms of chasmèd fears,
> From those strong Feet that followed, followed after.
>   But with unhurrying chase
>   And unperturbèd pace,
>   Deliberate speed, majestic instancy,
>   They beat — and a Voice beat
>   More instant than the Feet —
> "All things betray thee, who betrayest Me."[4]

But the apostle Paul, who years before on the Damascus road had taken his own trip down "titanic glooms of chasmèd fears," knew from personal experience that God's love invades such depths. That is why he cried in triumphant certainty that nothing "in all creation," not even "depth," is finally "able to separate us from the love of God in Christ Jesus our Lord" (Rom. 8:39, RSV). After all, his own Bible bore witness to the discovery of the psalmist:

> Whither shall I go from thy Spirit?
> Or whither shall I flee from thy presence?
> If I ascend to heaven, thou art there!
> If I make my bed in Sheol [that is, the abode of
>   the dead, the place where people perish],
>   thou art there! (Ps. 139:7-8, RSV).

2

On what can we base our confidence that love is like a "Hound of Heaven" barking at our heels on the outer boundaries of life? The New Testament answer is both clear and consistent: The cross of Christ is proof positive that God grapples with our perishing condition in the depths of life (Rom. 5:8). For Calvary is the culmination both of our own propensity to perish and of God's condescending love.

Consider first the cross as an absolute assertion of our determination to self-destruct. Has there ever been a more monstrous moment in human history? Here was a young man who sought only to offer his people "the kingdom of God," but, because he would not bow to nationalistic fanaticism, the cries of the fickle crowd swiftly changed from "Hosanna!" to "Crucify him!" He gathered no armies and allowed no swords, yet Roman justice was swayed to declare him — of all persons in that hotbed of Zealotism! — an enemy of Caesar. His only crime was to press the divine claim with unflinching authority, but the penalty for such "extremism" was capital punishment.

Look at the perpetrators of this ghastly deed: men with the blood of heaven on their hands trying to drive a dagger in God's back — blind, irrational, senseless, mad! And yet, the closer we look, the clearer it becomes that, but for time and circumstance, it could have been any of us! The villains in our plot were not hardened criminals or moral reprobates. Instead, they were the typical power structure which can be found guarding the status quo in almost any religious and political establishment to this day. Calvary does not condemn "The Jews" or "The Romans" or any other collective scapegoat for this miscarriage of justice. Rather, it exposes with relentless honesty how a representative cross section of human life can go utterly to hell in less than a week any time it decides to "love the darkness" and "hate the light" (John 3:19-20, AT).

But if here human hate came to its fiercest focus, it is also true that divine love came to its finest flower. Christ could have recoiled from the horror which he knew awaited him — that is what Gethsemane was all about (see Mark 14:32-42). Instead, he resolutely allowed the downswing of the "a parabola of redemption" (see Phil. 2:6-11) to bottom out in the noonday darkness of total dereliction (see Mark 15:34; 2 Cor. 5:21). His entire ministry had been an unforgettable epiphany of God's love, but now this divine wooing reached a climax at Calvary. Here God dressed himself out in crimson garments and came to court the love of every person.

The tragic pathos of that moment must not obscure the simple meaning of the event. Calvary demonstrated that Jesus would rather die than renounce his love for those whose lovelessness had driven them to the point of perishing. "Greater *love* has no man than this, that a man lay down his life" (John 15:13, RSV, author's italics). "Having loved his own who were in the world, he *loved* them to the end" (John 13:1, RSV, author's italics). "By this we know *love*, that he laid down his life for us" (1 John 3:16, RSV, author's italics). In short, *Calvary meant that infinite love would pay the price of infinite pain to overcome the infinite distance between God and humankind*!

In her novel about Peter Abelard, the medieval saint and sinner, Helen Waddell tells of a time when Abelard and his friend Thibault were stopped in their tracks by a piercing scream of intolerable anguish. Rushing into the woods they found a rabbit, helplessly crushed in a trap, that breathed its last in Abelard's arms. Stung by the senselessness of such cruelty, Abelard cried out, "Do you think there is a God at all?" "I know," Thibault nodded, "Only—I think God is in it too." "In it?" answered Abelard. "Do you mean that it makes Him suffer...? Thibault, do you mean Calvary?" "Yes," replied his friend, "but that was only a piece of it—the piece that we saw—in time. Like that." Thibault pointed to a fallen tree beside them, sawed through the middle. "That dark ring there, it goes up and down the whole length of the tree. But you only see it where it is cut across."[5]

Calvary was that moment when, in the fullness of time, Christ revealed a "cross section" of the eternal love of God. We saw the dark spot of suffering only where his life was torn asunder, but the gospel announces that it goes up and down the whole length of human history. "Then, Thibault," Abelard mused, "you think that all this," he looked down at the mangled body in his arms, "all the pain of the world, was Christ's cross?" "God's cross," said Thibault. "And it goes on."[6]

Horace Bushnell spoke of that "cross in God before the wood is seen upon Calvary"[7] when he said:

> Nay, if we will let our plummet down to the bottom of this great sea, the cross of Jesus represents and reveals the tremendous cross that is hid in the bosom of God's love and life from eternity.[8]

We are now in a position to sound the depths of God's involvement in our perishing condition. When the Eternal acts in time, he acts for all time — which means both that we are contemporaries of Christ's cross and that Christ is contemporary with all our crosses. On the one hand, as the Negro spiritual has it, "We *were there*" when they crucified our Lord. But on the other hand, he *is here* as in a thousand different ways we crucify him afresh (see Heb. 6:6). And, in Luther's daring phrase, all of this has to do, not simply with the misfortune which befell an ancient Galilean prophet, but with the "Crucified God,"[9] with the never-ending vulnerability of divine love to human hurt. What Scripture means by saying that Christ was "destined" to shed his precious blood "before the foundation of the world" (1 Pet. 1:20, RSV) is that God reckoned with the tragic consequences of human freedom even before he created us and so decided, in advance, to gather up into himself all of the dying that we would ever deserve for our misdeeds.

In his book about the Jewish Holocaust, entitled

Night, Elie Wiesel describes God's contemporaneity with our crosses:

> The SS hanged two Jewish men and a youth in front of the whole camp. The men died quickly, but the death throes of the youth lasted for half an hour. "Where is God? Where is he?" someone asked behind me. As the youth still hung in torment in the noose after a long time, I heard the man call again, "Where is God now?" And I heard a voice in myself answer: "Where is he? He is here. He is hanging there on the gallows."[10]

Add to those gallows all the inhumanity that man has ever visited upon his fellowman in all ages and you will begin to realize not only our incredible capacity for lovelessness (perishing) but God's even more incredible capacity for suffering love (saving). Having said that, however, there is a limit to our penetration of such an abyss. When the great polar explorer, Fridtjof Nansen, was sounding the depths of the Arctic seas, he came one day to a spot where all his line would not touch bottom. After the last foot had been played out, every piece of rope and cord on deck was added, then sheets were ripped into strips that were tied to the line. Still the plummet did not rest on the bottom. Nansen recorded in his log the total depth fathomed, then added: "Deeper yet."[11]

In search of the depth of God's love, we may tie together every tear, every cry, every pain of human heartbreak. But still our line will not touch bottom, for

None of the ransomed ever knew
How deep were the waters crossed;
Nor how dark was the night that the Lord passed thro'
Ere He found His sheep that was lost.[12]

Finally, then, we must write "deeper yet" over all our explorations of "the depths of God" (1 Cor. 2:10, RSV), content to claim the promise of John 3:16 that perishing need not be our ultimate lot. For, as another stanza puts it:

> Through all the depths of sin and loss
> Drops the plummet of the cross;
> Never yet abyss was found
> Deeper than the cross can sound![13]

3

Unable to probe more deeply the divine side of that event on Calvary, we may turn now to the human side and ask what it means to respond to such invincible love. Two essential insights are conveyed by the familiar *de profundis* of the psalmist, "Out of the *depths* I cry to thee, O Lord!" (Ps. 130:1, RSV, author's italics). One is the honest confession that we have tumbled into an abyss from which we cannot extricate ourselves. The other is the sure confidence that God will hear us from that humiliating pit of despair. Centuries later, a German mystic clarified how both of these convictions could be true: "Oh, who will give me a voice that I may cry aloud to the whole world that God, the all-highest, is in the deepest abyss within us and is waiting for us to return to him!"[14]

Here is the profoundest paradox at the heart of the gospel, that those who flee the farthest from God are actually running into the arms of God. For it is precisely those who reenact Calvary as the epitome of their lovelessness who hear most clearly his declaration of love, "Father, forgive them; for they know not what they do" (Luke 23:34, KJV). It was this truth to which Dietrich Bonhoeffer bore witness when he said, "the world is more godless, and perhaps it is for that very reason *nearer to God* than ever before."[15] The words echo Luther: "Nobody in this life is nearer God than those who hate and blaspheme him. He has no more dear children than they."[16]

When I served as pastor of the congregation to which this book is dedicated, my study was located on the second floor of an educational building, approachable by a flight of stairs which led directly to the door. One hot summer morning I heard shuffling footfalls followed by a timid knock. It was a man about forty-five years of age whom "the Hounds of Heaven" had at bay. No sooner was he seated than he began to pour out a tale of woe: chronic alcoholism, divorce, business failure, loss of reputation. I suspect that the momentum of this confessional carried him to a level of candor which he had not intended, making him painfully aware of the stark contrast between his wasted life and my rather sheltered circumstances as pastor of a respected church. Sensing my distance from the sordid world in which he had been living, he reached forward and grasped the edge of the desk until his knuckles showed white. This time he fairly spit the words in my face:

"Preacher, you don't understand what I'm talking about. *I've been to hell!*"

"True," I responded, "I have had no firsthand experience with any of your wretched escapades. But I am not here to save you. You say you've been to hell. Let me tell you about somebody who went to hell to bring you back." Then I led that startled man to Calvary, where men made a hell if ever it has erupted on this earth. I showed him how the strong Son of God loved those who had betrayed life far more perversely than he had ever contemplated. And I added, "You say that you have hit rock bottom. Look again, that just might be the Rock of Ages. For the miracle of divine love is that when man is at his sinning worst, God is at his saving best!"

That morning, another desperate man discovered that when we can neither love, nor be loved by, others, God will love us still. Francis Thompson found it out when his running days were over, and he heard God say:

> Alack, thou knowest not
> How little worthy of any love thou art!
> Whom wilt thou find to love ignoble thee
>   Save Me, save only Me?
> All which I took from thee I did but take,
>   Not for thy harms,
> But just that thou might'st seek it in My arms.[17]

This way of being saved does not leave us passive recipients of a relentless love that will not be denied. Rather, the shock of discovering what *agape*-love can do for our lives impels us to love others in the same daring fashion (1 John 4:7-12). It is not enough simply to love God in gratitude for his love to us. That would not be loving as he first loved us. It would not be taking the initiative, as God did, but only reacting to his love. It would not be loving the unlovely, as God did, but loving the loveliest one of all! No, only as we take the initiative and surprise our unlovely neighbor with love do we show in action that we really understand what God's love is all about.

After Bishop Booth of Vermont died, his nurse said to a friend, "I know where the Bishop is tonight. His soul has gone to hell!" The friend was too shocked to speak, so the nurse continued, "That's the only place he can be happy; there's such work to do there."[18] We need not wait for our demise to begin living like that, for hell happens anywhere that "saving love goes out to undergird this life of ours, and comes back with the hot stab of nails in its hands."[19] But we, like our Lord, may use our crosses to declare the true "depth" of God's love. It goes to hell that no one need perish even there!

Mebane Ramsey of Hagerman, New Mexico, has told of a group of visitors being shown through the labyrinthine passageways of the Carlsbad Caverns. As they wound their way to the deepest point in the caves, all of the lights were turned out in order that the group might experience total blackness, unrelieved by a single ray from sun or moon. So intense and overwhelming was the darkness that a seven-year-old girl began to whimper and cry. Bravely, her eleven-year-old brother placed his arm around her and whispered, "Don't you cry, little sister. There's someone down here who can turn the lights on."[20]

We can avoid neither the depths of life nor the darkness that may overwhelm us there. But in Jesus Christ we have found the one down here who can turn the lights on!

Notes

1. Adapted from Paul Scherer, *Love Is a Spendthrift* (New York: Harper & Brothers, 1961), p. 32.

2. Smiley Blanton, *Love or Perish* (New York: Simon and Schuster, 1956).

3. "Personal Glimpses," *The Reader's Digest*, February, 1976, pp. 33-34, from Hiram Haydn, *Words & Faces*, who decided to work for Cerf at Random House after happening to hear him on this program.

4. Francis Thompson, "The Hound of Heaven," *Masterpieces of Religious Verse*, ed. James Dalton Morrison (New York: Harper & Brothers, 1948), p. 57.

5. Helen Waddell, *Peter Abelard* (New York: Henry Holt, 1933), pp. 288-290. Summarized in Archibald M. Hunter, *Interpreting Paul's Gospel* (Philadelphia: Westminster, 1955), p. 90.

6. Waddell, p. 290.

7. Quoted without documentation in Vincent Taylor, *The Cross of Christ* (London: Macmillan, 1956), pp. 8, 75.

8. Horace Bushnell, *The Vicarious Sacrifice* (London: Alexander Strahan, 1866), p. 259.

9. For a major theological treatise on this theme see Jurgen Moltmann, *The Crucified God* (New York: Harper & Row, 1974).

10. Elie Wiesel, *Night*, 1969, pp. 75-76; quoted in Moltmann, pp. 273-274.

11. Robert C. Shannon, "Let Me Illustrate," *Pulpit Digest*, July-August, 1978, p. 32.

12. Elizabeth C. Clephane, "The Ninety and Nine," stanza 3.

13. Cited by Shannon, p. 32.

14. Quoted without attribution by Edward W. Bauman, *The Life and Teaching of Jesus* (Philadelphia: Westminster, 1960), p. 134.

15. Dietrich Bonhoeffer, *Letters and Papers from Prison*, 3rd. ed., rev. and enlarg., ed. Eberhard Bethge (London: SCM, 1967), p. 200. I have here followed the translation in Harvey Cox, *The Secular City*, rev. ed. (New York: Macmillan, 1966), pp. 71-72. In the original context, Bonhoeffer was making a somewhat different point about "the world that has come of age," whereas I have sought only to sharpen the paradox of God in the midst of our godlessness. For a theological analysis, see Gerhard Eberling, *Word and Faith* (London: SCM, 1963), pp. 130-132, esp. n. 4.

16. Quoted by Scherer, p. 71.

17. Thompson, p. 70.

18. Harry Emerson Fosdick, *A Great Time to Be Alive* (New York: Harper & Brothers, 1944), p. 79.

19. Scherer, p. 81. (This must have been a favorite saying of Scherer, for he repeated it on p. 155!)

20. Halford E. Luccock and Robert E. Luccock, "Springboards For Sermons," *Pulpit Digest*, July, 1955, p. 38.

V
The Height of
God's Love

In the west-central section of our land lies an invisible but significant line called the Continental Divide. Running along a ridge of mountain summits, it marks the boundary between streams that flow eastward toward the Mississippi River and those that flow westward toward the Pacific Ocean. Although water may fall from the same sky and collect at almost the same point, this fateful median determines whether it shall move in opposite directions and so reach completely different destinations.

We come now to that Great Divide in our scaling of the Mount Everest of Christian truth: "should not perish *but* have eternal life" (John 3:16*d*, RSV, author's italics). That simple connective "but" traces the watershed of human existence. On one side—*perishing*; on the other side—*living*. This means that life is fundamentally a matter of choice between two absolute alternatives. There is no middle ground between the mutually exclusive options of destruction or preservation.[1] Although we may all approach our text in the same human condition, the ultimate implications of our response to its claim are as different as moving eastward is from moving westward.

The apostle Paul insisted that we ponder a fourth and final dimension: the "height" of God's love (Eph. 3:18). And so we ask our all-sufficient text, "What can love do for persons whom it reaches in the depths of perishing?" Faithfully John 3:16 replies, "It can lift them to the heights of eternal life!" Coiled up in that little conjunction on which this last phrase pivots is the hinge of human destiny. Over against the decay and stench of all our perishing, the gospel sets a divine disjunctive, the possibility of a fresh start, the option of reversing an otherwise inevitable fate. In one brief but breathtaking construction — *not* this *but* that! — the climax of our key verse describes how love reaches down to Calvary for the forlorn creatures gathered there and, instead of crushing them, flings them against the canopy of heaven.

1

The contrast between these two conditions could not be greater. For perishing, by its nature, is seen as something done and over, life impaled on a point, a squandering until there is nothing left to waste, a casting of all that is of value to the void. But eternal life is seen as an abiding sense of fulfillment, existence that is an enduring permanent possession with a built-in vitality whose momentum is never spent. The meaning inherent in the two contrasting verbs sharpens the force of the forms in which they are found here, suggesting the paraphrase: "should not come to a dead end with everything utterly lost but, instead, continue to enjoy eternal life with open-ended duration."[2]

This discovery of a durable existence is summarized in the Johannine description of salvation as something that we "have." The present tense of this verb points to the possession of eternal life as far more than a future hope. In so doing, it identifies the Christian faith as a religion of *having* rather than as one of seeking or expecting.[3] The claim being made is that in the coming of Jesus Christ into our world all the richness of what it means to be loved by God has entered into the here-and-now. Christianity has to do not with dreams but with reality, not with expectations but with fulfillment, not with tomorrow but with today. It is not that we can face the present because of what we are sure will come in the future. Rather, we can face the future with confidence because of what we are sure has already come in the present!

Let us explore, in a bit more detail, the two chief characteristics of a religion of "having," its givenness and its presentness. First, to say that eternal life is something that we "have" underscores its nature as a gift from God. The simple verb "to have" may also be translated "to hold," a meaning which beautifully balances our passivity and our activity in response to the divine initiative. On the one hand, "to have and to hold" anything requires that we be open and willing to receive it. There is no place here for coercion, manipulation, or intrigue. On the other hand, once we receive what is offered, it becomes our responsibility to be good stewards of that which is given to us in trust. In a word, to say that we "have" eternal life implies that we are grateful custodians of a gift rather than proud conquerors of a prize.

In a profound sense, then, "to have" is the only appropriate verb with which to describe our acceptance of God's love. Even at the human level, it is not accidental that when a bride and groom give themselves to each other they promise "to *have* and to *hold* from this day forward...." For love, by its nature, is destroyed if forced. Its fragile presence is shattered by the squeeze of a compulsive grasp. We cannot clutch love, or exploit love, or demand love. We can only "have" love and "hold" love in thanksgiving that it has been given to us.

If that be true of all human loves, how much more is it true of divine love. In chapter III we learned that God gave his only beloved Son as a "present" to demonstrate his love for all the world. In the face of that gift, we dare not claim that we sought it or earned it or deserve it but only that we "have" it!

Second, to the mystery of the givenness of God's love, which was simply *there for the having* when we expected it least, is added the mystery of its presentness in a world where, otherwise, everything perishes. There is here no hint of equivocation, as if we "will," or "should," or "may," or "might" someday escape our plight. Instead, there is only the categorical declaration: *"does now have* eternal life." It has always been easy for us to imagine a future utopia, either as the result of religious bliss or as the projection of our human fantasies. Nor can there be much basis for argument with such dreams, since their realization is yet to come, except to complain that they are all mere speculation. But to insist that believers actually *have* eternal life here and now is something entirely different. For that kind of claim can be tested by its effect on daily life. Christianity dares to put forth an eschatology that can be experienced and not just expected!

But note the implications of affirming that some already "have" eternal life in the midst of a situation where others are already perishing (see John 3:36). This means that the most enduring realities coexist in our world with those that are the most transitory, and this is because an entirely new order has invaded the old order *without replacing it.* Instead, a dialectical situation is created in which the "haves" and the "have nots," in respect to eternal life, still live together on planet Earth. Such an arrangement represents a transformation of the segmented and sequential eschatology of Judaism according to which the New Age would not come until the Old Age had passed away. What we are being told here is that love does not work by cosmic catastrophe but slips unobtrusively into our world one heart at a time. Despite its complete absence of ostentation, however, such love brings with it nothing less than a whole new realm of existence as deathless as the life of God himself.

2

When we inquire more closely just what it is that we "have" as a result of God's love, the answer of our text is "life." Could any reality be more all-embracing? Life encompasses every facet of our being; every memory, every aspiration, every relationship, every time, every place. How much larger the very definition of religion becomes when measured by this norm. No longer a Sunday observance but a week-long life-style. No longer a set of pious practices, such as prayer and Bible study, but all of the deeds that comprise the daily round. No longer those activities which take place in the church facilities but the whole complex of acts and attitudes by which we express ourselves at work and play. John 3:16 insists that Christianity is either as large as life or it is not Christianity at all!

Because such life is said to be our present possession in a world that is perishing, we might suppose that only "spiritual" life is meant, in the sense of an etherealized mystical inwardness. But the emphasis in the Gospel of John is on the full range of concrete existence that enters completely into the historical process.[4] That emphasis is rooted in the nature of the incarnation by which God's "Word" of love to mankind in his beloved Son "became flesh" (John 1:14, RSV). Quite simply, Jesus manifested the Father's love in the totality of his whole-orbed existence: every word that he spoke, every deed that he did, every emotion that he felt. He was "*full* of grace and truth" (John 1:14, RSV, author's italics); that is, love filled every crevice of his life. And "of that *fulness* we receive" (John 1:16, AT), which means that no crevice of our life is exempt from the change wrought by his love.

The claim here in John 3:16, therefore, represents the climax of two other claims of Jesus. First, "*I* am the life" (John 14:6, AT), and second, "I came that *you* may have life" (John 10:10, AT). In other words, to say that we have "life" is but another way of saying that we have Christ. He embodied authentic existence because he knew what it meant to be fully loved by God, and the whole point of his ministry was to share with us a realization of that same love. But Jesus did not live in a charmed circle, free from the unloveliness of this world. Hence the gift of his life carries with it no implication that we may enjoy some better fate. If Christ could live true life in Nazareth and Jerusalem, then he can help us to live it wherever we may be.

The key contention here in relation to the totality of our text is that perishing existence may be transformed into durable existence because of the extravagant way in which God loved us by giving up his only Son. Put very simply, now we can *really live* because we have been *really loved*! The unique connection between life and love is already clear from ordinary experience. Someone spurns us through criticism, opposition, or outright rejection and, in the denial of love, *we feel like dying*! But let someone accept us with affirmation, affection, or even adoration and, in the gift of that love, *we feel like living*! Whenever love is reciprocated, something quickens within us that suffuses the totality of our being. Circumstances may not alter, resources may not increase, problems may not disappear, but suddenly we can face our situation with a new vitality that betokens the upsurge of life deep within.

Why should this be so? Because love lures us away from that self-centeredness which is mired, at one extreme, in pride, smugness, and conceit, or, at the other extreme, in weakness, insecurity, and fear. Egocentricity, by its nature, results in a rigid, closed, dead-end existence; whereas love, by its na-

ture, calls us to reciprocity, to sharing, and hence to
an open-ended existence. To love because we have
been loved creates a two-way channel that allows us
to draw life from life. When tied to others by bonds
of affection, we are delivered from the lonely abyss
of never really mattering to anybody. We are no
longer tempted to be secure-in-ourselves, because
now we know that the best things in life are gifts
from others. Nor are we any longer tempted to be
insecure-in-ourselves, because now we know that
someone else cares for us just as we are.

By establishing the inherent connection between
love and life, John 3:16 reinforces the twin truths: "I
love in order to live," and "I live in order to love."
But our text lifts these axioms to an ultimate level
by rooting love in the sovereign initiative of God.
We must now examine more closely what this involves, for it is just here that we discover what it
means to say that our life in Christ is "eternal."

3

What happens when we take all that we have
been able to learn about the healing power of love
and relate it not just to our immediate family and
most intimate friends but to the Lord of the whole
universe? We have already learned that, in giving
his only beloved Son, God offered his heart to every
person being destroyed for lack of love. Because that
agape-love proved inexhaustible when put to the
supreme test at Calvary, we may dare to believe that
the life based upon it will prove inexhaustible as
well. Even the best of human loves sometimes

proves fickle, as when a spouse forsakes the vows of a lifetime because love has turned to ashes. But the constancy of God's love is our assurance that life will never fail because his "love never fails" (1 Cor. 13:8, AT).

This durability of divine love is underscored in our text by the addition of the adjective "everlasting" (KJV) or "eternal" (RSV). The primary connotation of this modifier is not quantitative but qualitative, not "everlasting" in the sense of endless in measure but "eternal" in the sense of ultimate in meaning. As such, it is a virtual synonym for that which is divine. "Eternal life . . . is the life that God lives and that he imparts to his creatures in the act of loving them."[5] The terminology itself is most literally translated "the life of the age" (*zōē aiōnios*), that long-awaited era when human existence was to be transformed by the redemptive work of God. In one sense, the explosion of love in the historical ministry of Jesus launched a whole new order in the midst of the old. All of those who discover Christ's love may enter immediately, in advance as it were, into that realm of true fulfillment.

Unfortunately, the traditional translation "everlasting" has popularized a mistaken emphasis on mere endlessness, as if the primary point of our text is that we will live forever in heaven. Actually, however, the promise here is not that one day something endless will stretch out before us, but that right now we may reach the end of all our strivings. When we find personal fulfillment by appropriating God's love, life is no longer end-*less* but, if anything, is end-*full* in the sense that nothing greater is yet to come because "the greatest thing in the world" is already here!

At the same time, there is a temporal dimension to this new age of love in which we may now live, for that which is eternal does transcend the limitations of time. Consider for a moment the profound connection between love and time. By its very nature as personal and relational, love always needs more time for cultivation than we ever have available to give it here on earth. How often do we lament that there was never enough time really to learn to love our children or our neighbors or our fellow church members. If anything, the wonders of modern transportation and communication have thrust us into a host of superficial relationships with no opportunity to explore most of them in any depth. How frustrated we feel when death cheats us of the chance to get to know intimately someone whom we had yearned to love. In a strange sense, we finally discover that even a whole lifetime is not long enough to exhaust the potentialities of loving just one other person!

In the face of a temporal finitude that deeply compromises our capacity for true affection, the offer of eternal life holds out the promise that we will finally have enough time to love! Far from being an unending monotony, the eternity that has already begun here on earth will offer us a boundless opportunity to love without any of the limits imposed by our temporal existence. In one sense, any life grounded in love needs to be eternal because it is the nature of love to be inexhaustible. Our hunch that love always has an unfinished agenda, even when confined to a

few selected relationships here on earth, is but one
authentic intimation that heaven will be a life of un-
limited growth in love. When 1 Corinthians 13 talks
about love "never ending" and "always abiding"
(vv. 8-13, AT), what it means is that love is the one
reality that it will literally take us forever fully to
enjoy!

The poet Arthur Vine Hall pictured the pioneer
missionary explorer David Livingstone "At the Victoria Falls" in the heart of central Africa as he
sought to trace the Zambesi to its issue.

"Where goes the river?" Livingstone enquired.
  Then did a dusky Solomon declare,
  With naked dignity and learned air:
"White Chief, the knowledge many have desired
We give to you. It is a lion tired
  By a great leap, who seeks afar his lair,
  Sleeps, and by sand is covered; none know where."
Thus the witch-doctor, confident, inspired.

Th' intrepid Traveller thought otherwise.
  Ever he journeyed on undauntedly.
Not years of loneliness; nor nightly cries —
  Perils of man and beast; not agony
Of burning days of fever and of flies
  Deterring; till, at last — "The sea, the sea!"[6]

Many in our world today view life as a winding
river that, tired from its earthly struggles, finally
rounds the last bend only to sleep in the sands of
time, "none know where." But just as David Livingstone discovered that the Zambesi did not disappear
into the desert but was gathered up into the great

Indian Ocean, so the person who has discovered
God's love in Jesus Christ knows that, no matter
how insignificant his or her life may be, when it
finally rounds the last bend it will not run out into
the sand but will be gathered up into the great ocean
of God's love. That is why we sing:

> O Love that wilt not let me go,
> I rest my weary soul in thee;
> I give thee back the life I owe,
> That in thine *ocean depths* its flow
> May richer, fuller be.[7]

Notes

1. C. K. Barrett, *The Gospel According to St. John*
(London: S.P.C.K., 1955), p. 180.

2. Many commentators have called attention to the
temporal contrast between the aorist *apolētai* ("should
not perish once-for-all") and the present *echē* ("have with
abiding present enjoyment"). So B. F. Westcott, *The Gospel According to St. John* (London: James Clarke, 1958
reprint), p. 55.

3. Hermann Hanse, *"echō,"* *Theological Dictionary
of the New Testament*, ed. by Gerhard Kittel (Grand
Rapids: Wm. B. Eerdmans, 1964), 2:818, 825-827.

4. Rudolph Bultmann, *"zaō,"* ibid., 2:870-871.

5. C. H. Dodd, "Eternal Life," *Harvard Divinity
School Bulletin*, (1950-51), 16:15.

6. Arthur Vine Hall, "At the Victoria Falls," *Poems of
a South African*, cited in R. J. Campbell, *Livingstone*
(Westport, Connecticut: Greenwood Press, 1972 reprint),
p. xiv.

7. George Matheson, "O Love That Wilt Not Let Me
Go," stanza 1.

VI
The Ultimate Dimension

Looking at the four dimensions of God's love sketched in Ephesians 3:18 and given substance in John 3:16, what spacious vistas have unfolded before our eyes! In every direction we have discovered that the Everlasting Mercy fills our universe, leaving us no escape from its reality and claim.

But any sphere, no matter how vast its circumference, proceeds from a fixed center. Therefore, having looked outward at the objective dimensions of God's love, we need now to look inward at the subjective dimension which enables us to internalize a universe of love in one human heart and so to get a "focus on infinity"[1] in each individual life. Only as we learn how to let love fill the little world of selfhood will we be "filled with all the fulness of God" that knows no bounds (Eph. 3:19, AT).

Consistent with its comprehensiveness at every other point, John 3:16 also gives adequate definition to this final dimension in its one remaining phrase which we have not yet considered, "that whoever believes in him." Paul anticipated this crucial connection between divine love and human faith in his Ephesian prayer by suggesting, in successive clauses, that, when Christ dwells in our hearts "through *faith*" (3:17*a*), we are thereby rooted and grounded "in *love*" (3:17*b*, RSV, author's italics). Let us now draw out the significance of this linkage between faith and love established by our two primary passages.

1

At first it seems incredible that both John and Paul would identify faith as the one and only condition for claiming God's love. For that love is nothing less than ultimate reality, yet these apostles dared to insist that it is available to anyone who will accept it by faith. Even though few things are as fragile or even fickle as human faith, this tiny key is said to unlock the immensities of heaven's treasures. In the face of life's finest offer, we are bidden, not to think or to plan or to work, but only to believe!

Rather than cheapening divine love, however, this surprising connection serves to ennoble the meaning of faith. For it suggests that, at bottom, faith is not mere credulity, a kind of simplistic naïveté in the face of baffling perplexity, a wistful surmise that everything will somehow come out all right in the end. Instead, the essence of faith is a willingness to be loved, to encounter *agape* in the abyss of life, to face all the wonder and terror of human existence locked in an unbreakable embrace with God! Stated as simply as possible, *faith is our human response to the wooing of divine love.* But why should we be asked to respond to God in faith rather than in love?

Throughout the present study we have repeatedly

emphasized two truths about God's love that stand in profound tension. (1) By its very nature, love yearns for reciprocity; indeed, it requires a response of love in order to be fulfilled. (2) Yet, there is so fundamental a discrepancy between God's selfless love of the world and the world's selfish love of darkness that no such reciprocity is possible on a natural basis. Therefore, John 3:16 does not ask us to *love* God in return for his love to us, as if the verse read: "God so loved the world that we ought to love him back and thereby be saved." Rather, it asks us to have *faith* in God's love for us declared uniquely in Jesus Christ. That love stands outside of us as a prior "given" which we may embrace regardless of any inability to love God on our own.

To ask us to be saved by loving God in response to his love for us is an exercise in futility, because our affections have been alienated by the world (John 3:19). As children of darkness, we are incapable of authentic love, and there is no good news in being told that the requirement for salvation is the one thing that we cannot do precisely because of the predicament from which we need to be saved! Instead, good news comes in being told that *when we are not yet able to love God on our own, at least we can believe that God has already loved us on his own!* Such faith opens our loveless lives to the presence of Christ. Then, slowly but surely, we learn how to respond to God's love guided by the perfect love of his only Son. In other words, our ability to love God authentically becomes not the *condition* but the *consequence* of salvation, the fruit of Christ's Spirit working within our hearts (see Gal. 5:22).

2

Having clarified the unique connection between love and faith, let us look now at each of these realities in the light of the other. We may begin with a fresh look at love in relation to faith. As already implied in these chapters, the central issue of existence is not *whether* to love but *what* to love. By placing the option of faith at its very center, John 3:16 insists that, if finally we perish, it is entirely our fault and not the result of any desire on the part of God to be destructive. "For God sent not his Son into the world to condemn the world; but that the world through him might be saved" (John 3:17, KJV). Divine judgment is in no sense vindictive but is simply the crisis in which we decide on the loves of our life. For his part, God sees to it that we are confronted with ultimate alternatives, but beyond that he leaves to us the choice of where we will lodge our affections — salvation or condemnation issuing inevitably from that decision. "This is the judgment, that the light has come into the world, and men loved darkness rather than light, because their deeds were evil" (John 3:19, RSV).

Based on the close linkage between love and faith established in John 3:16, there is in the Fourth Gospel a well-developed understanding according to which belief is profoundly affected by true or false affections. Faith leads to authentic love which, in turn, deepens and supports that faith. Conversely, lack of faith leads to self-love which, in turn, impedes the possibility of faith. In short, what we believe affects what we love and what we love affects what we believe!

In Johannine thought, the two great competitors for our love are the Father above and the world below (1 John 2:15). If we refuse to accept God's love, it is because we love the world instead. But if we believe in Christ and so receive the love of God into our lives, we can no longer give our affections to the world. Actually, only God can love "the world" in any positive sense (John 3:16) since he alone is free from its corrupting temptations. For those of us susceptible to "the lust of the flesh and the lust of the eyes and the pride of life" (1 John 2:16, RSV), these two loves are irreconcilable. Let us examine in a bit more detail what it means to love the Father versus what it means to love the world, beginning with the latter.[2]

There are at least three components to that love of the world which thwarts our appropriation of God's love by faith: (1) The first of these, found in the immediate context of our key verse, is "love of darkness" (John 3:19, AT). Just as criminals relish the cover of night because the natural light would expose their evil deeds, so sinners enjoy life without the spiritual light of Christ (John 8:12; 9:5) "because their works are wicked" when measured by his goodness. (2) At the close of the public ministry, the cowardice of many Jewish authorities in refusing to confess Jesus is attributed to a "love for the glory of men" (John 12:43, AT). Even among religious leaders, the desire for peer group approval and the advancement which it confers is so strong that some seek to be exalted by men rather than by God (see also John 5:41-44; 7:18, 8:50). (3) A final kind of culpable affection is described as "love for one's own life" (John 12:25, AT). The paradoxical form of the saying in which this love is defined suggests that it signifies a sparing of self from any demands for renunciation.

Over against this negative love of the world, the Fourth Gospel also describes a positive love of the Father in threefold fashion: (1) Love for the glory of God (John 12:43), a desire for divine honor both to be bestowed by God on man and to be given to God from man, exactly as the Son was glorified by the Father and the Father by the Son (John 11:4; 12:23,28; 13:31-32; 17:1,4-5); (2) Love for the light (John 3:19), an openness to God's disclosure of himself in the luminous life of his Son; (3) Love for Christ (John 8:42), an affinity based on a common spiritual heredity, God being the heavenly Father of both.

Thomas Barrosse has provided a useful summary of the perspectives in these texts:

> In Christ God offers Himself to men out of love. Christ is the concrete manifestation of God's love in the world. To believe in Christ means to accept Him as God's offer of Himself; in other words, it means to comply with the advances of God's love. Those who love themselves inordinately, who desire a glory independent of the borrowed glory they can have from God in Christ or who love the evil which they have apart from God, can only reject the offer of God's love and refuse to believe. Only those who love God's glory and who therefore love Christ, the manifestation and offer of that glory, will accept the advances of God's love. These are the [ones] who have the "love of God" within them.[3]

3

Having looked in some detail at love in relation to faith, let us now look more closely at faith in relation to love. Faith has many facets because it involves the total process by which a person responds to the saving presence of God in human life. Stated as simply as possible, this response may be said to have three great movements which we will now isolate for purposes of analysis even though, in actual experience, they are inextricably intertwined. The most interesting thing to notice for our purposes is that all three components are, at bottom, an affair of the heart. That is why, as we shall see in each case, the clearest analogies come from our most intimate involvement with love, such as the marital relationship.

(1) The first strand of saving faith is what we may call *confidence in Christ* as worthy of all that we can offer him. The initial step in this direction involves an element of credence, the conviction that Christ's claims are actually true. But once the credibility gap has been bridged, then "believing *that*" certain affirmations are authoritative leads on to "believing *in*" those realities at the level of personal assurance. The new element here is trust, a shift from knowledge *about* to acceptance *of*, so that what were merely facts become a foundation on which we are willing to stand.[4] This connotation of faith is captured by a legitimate translation of our phrase in John 3:16 as "that whoever believes *upon* him" in the sense of casting one's whole being upon Christ as utterly trustworthy.[5]

Today we hear much about a credibility gap of

crisis proportions, reflecting a low level of confidence in many of our public leaders because their
claims do not always turn out to be true. After
Watergate, for example, the trust level in the U.S.
presidency plummeted as flagrant examples of deliberate deception became common knowledge. The
resulting cynicism about self-serving politicans
makes us wary of placing our future in the hands of
any would-be messiah. But Christ is credible as the
supreme leader of life because he cares deeply about
our well-being rather than his own self-interests.
There is not a trace of evidence from his earthly life
that he would ever exploit any of his followers for
selfish ends.

Nothing raises the confidence level in another person quite like love. When two people marry, for
example, they literally "swear by" each other as
worthy of a lifetime companionship because of the
intensity of their affections. Despite a past filled
with immaturity, and a future filled with uncer-
tainty, they dare to embark upon this adventure
together because of the "faith" which they have in
each other, a confidence inspired not by knowledge
or by experience but by love. The only thing that
can shake such a relationship is not adversity but
infidelity (literally, "un-faith"), which need not take
the form of overt adultery but may express itself as
a suspicion that destroys mutual confidence. In the
religious realm, "God is faithful" (1 Cor. 1:9; 10:13; 2
Tim. 2:13) in the sense of loving with a dependable
love which gives us the assurance that he will never
disappoint us.

(2) If confidence in the trustworthiness of Christ

represents the objective side of faith, then personal *commitment to Christ* represents its subjective dimension. Obviously, these two facets of faith are inseparably related. It is only because Christ proves himself worthy of complete trust that we become willing to make an exclusive decision on his behalf. Negatively, this response involves a relinquishment of self-love, a repudiation of the darkness, a renunciation of the world. Positively, it involves an attachment to Christ, an obedience to his will, a willingness to follow wherever he may lead. Although this either/or dialectic of decision is decisively settled at the outset of discipleship, it should be renewed and thereby deepened at each stage of the pilgrimage.

Today, precisely because of our low level of confidence in so many leaders, we are reluctant to become absolutely committed to anyone. We forever hedge our bets, never quite resolving the issues of life in one grand wager. The most significant feature of contemporary political life, for example, is not rabid partisanship but wholesale apathy—the great majority taking neither side by refusing to vote![6]

But notice again how love enables us to make clean-cut choices. When approaching the option of marriage, for example, we may know many fine persons whose credentials are in order, whose character inspires confidence, and whose companionship would be meaningful for a lifetime. Finally, however, we decide to commit ourselves to only one person *instead of to anyone else* because of the exclusive nature of marital love. To hesitate perpetually between available options, or to defer a decision indefinitely in anticipation of other options not yet identified, would only demonstrate that we are not really in love and would thereby cause us to forfeit the possibility of marriage. In like manner, only an overriding devotion to Christ compels us to yield to him unreservedly as Lord of all life.

(3) The final characteristic of faith is, in one sense, a combination of the other two. When confidence in Christ becomes such that we can commit ourselves to him unconditionally, then the new relationship that results needs constantly to be cultivated. This maturation process leads to a sense of shared life which is best described in the Fourth Gospel by the concept of "abiding" (John 15:1-17). Many metaphors are used for this developing mutuality: the vine and the branches (15:1-11); the shepherd and the sheep (10:1-18); the eating of bread (6:25-59); and the drinking of water (4:13-14; 7:37-38). The purpose of these analogies is to describe the achievement of an intimacy which further defines faith, not only as confidence in Christ and commitment to Christ, but as *communion with Christ*.

How superficial are so many of our human relationships today! We sponsor "mixers" in an effort to overcome anonymity. We wear badges, join clubs, form neighborhood associations, but so little intimacy results. One of the few ways in which our hunger for meaningful mutuality is satisfied is through a healthy marriage. Here, in that long process by which "two become one" (Mark 10:8, AT), the reciprocity which is a hallmark of love is deeply fulfilled at the earthly level.

But it is also possible to experience that reciprocity eternally at the spiritual level. When Paul said that "love never fails" (1 Cor. 13:8, AT), he certainly did not mean that Christians never fail to be loving in their dealings with others. Rather, he meant that whenever we love Christ, he will never fail to love us back in return! For his love is inexhaustible, thus there are no limits to the intimacy which we may share in communion with him.

The last, and perhaps the greatest, thing to be said about faith is that it is a response to God's love which *any* person in the world may make. John could have said simply that "the one believing" in Christ has eternal life, but instead he added an all-embracing adjective meaning "everyone" (*pas*) in order to emphasize that there are no limits placed on who may so believe. There is a universality in that "whoever" which is commensurate with the universality of God's love. We might paraphrase the connection thus: "Because God loved *everybody* in the whole wide world, he gave *everybody* a chance to be saved by accepting that love."

Bennett Cerf captured the indiscriminate nature of God's offer in the story of an eight-year-old girl consigned to a Pennsylvania orphanage as a ward of the state. Painfully shy, unattractive, shunned by other children, regarded as a problem student by her teachers, she had already been transferred from two other "asylums" (as they were called in that day) and now the administration sought some pretext for getting rid of her once again. It was an ironclad rule that any communication from children in the institution to outsiders had to be approved by the director in advance. One afternoon, the little girl was observed stealing down to the main gate and hiding a letter in the branches of an overhanging tree. Soon the director and her assistant hurried down to the wall. Sure enough, the unauthorized note was visible through the branches of the tree. The director pounced on it and tore open the envelope, then, without speaking, passed the contents to her assistant. Scrawled there were these words: "To anybody who finds this: I love you."[7]

That story is a broken but faithful pointer to one who was hung on a tree outside the city wall for anyone to find. In one sense, his cross was God's way of saying to the most casual passerby, to soldiers who gambled and criminals who railed and cynics who jeered: "To *whoever* finds this: I love you!"

The present chapter has tried to clarify just how one may go about finding God's love-note called John 3:16, which was written in language that even a child can understand. And the answer is as simple as the offer: it is found *by faith*, which comes down to casting a deciding vote for Christ because he has outloved every other competitor for the lordship of our lives.

Out of the history of the proud state of Georgia comes a story many years after the Civil War when General John B. Gordon was a candidate for the Senate of the United States. It was the custom in that day to elect senators by a vote of the state legislature, and, on the appointed day, General Gordon was present in the assembly hall of the Georgia State House as the legislators prepared to cast their ballots. Numbered in that company was an old comrade-in-arms who had come to dislike the General and was determined to vote against him. Just before his name was reached in the roll call, his eyes fell upon a deep and jagged scar that marked the face of General Gordon, mute testimony to the valor of this brave leader. As his fellow soldier's name was called, the man stood and hesitated; then, in a voice that was quiet but filled with emotion, said, "I cannot vote against him; I had forgotten the scar."[8]

T. H. Huxley once remarked, "I cannot see one shadow or tittle of evidence that God is love."[9] Nor will any of us ever quite see that evidence in its fullness until, as Paul prayed, we "comprehend" the four-dimensional love described by John 3:16. Nothing short of faith is sufficient to grasp the incredible truth that the love described there is what Calvary was all about. Beholding the nail-scarred hands of Christ in the light of John 3:16, understanding begins to dawn as we whisper, "I cannot vote against him. I had forgotten the scar."

Notes

1. The phrase is adapted from the title of a biography of Phillips Brooks by Raymond W. Albright, *Focus On Infinity* (New York: Macmillan, 1961).

2. This analysis follows Thomas Barrosse, "The Relationship of Love to Faith in St. John," *Theological Studies* 18 (1957):538-559.

3. Barrosse, p. 559

4. For philosophical reflections on the difference between "believing *that*" and "believing *in*," see Gabriel Marcel, *The Mystery of Being* (London: Harvell, 1951), 2:72-79.

5. H. W. Watkins, *The Gospel According to St. John* (London: Cassell, 1902), p. 82, who notes that the preposition for "believes *in*" in v. 16 (*eis*) is not the same as the preposition for "believes in" (*en*) in v. 15.

6. Kirkpatrick Sale, *Human Scale* (New York: Coward, McCann & Geoghegan, 1980), p. 25: "From 1966 to 1977, the Harris polls show that public confidence in the presidency dropped from 41 percent to 23 percent, in the Congress from 42 percent to 17 percent. Only 53 percent of the eligible voters bothered to go to the polls in the 1976 presidential election, and the percentage has been declining since 1960, although the number of eligible voters has been increased by 17 percent; 41 million voted for Carter, 39 million voted for Ford, and 66 million stayed home."

7. Recounted by Bennett Cerf in the *This Week* Sunday newspaper supplement of 1960 and reprinted in *Guideposts*, January, 1963, p. 7.

8. Recounted by Charles Wellborn, "Life at a Price," *The Baptist Hour* (Fort Worth: SBC Radio and Television Commission, March 5, 1950), p. 2.

9. Quoted by John Short, "The First Epistle to the Corinthians: Exposition," *The Interpreter's Bible*, ed. George Arthur Buttrick, 12 vols. (New York: Abingdon, 1951-57), 10:226.